DISCOVERING DINOSAURS

AN UP-TO-DATE GUIDE INCLUDING THE NEWEST THEORIES

By Victoria Crenson

*Illustrated by Robert Walters
and James Seward*

PRICE STERN SLOAN, INC.
Los Angeles

CONTENTS

1 DINOSAUR BONES   5

2 WHAT IS A DINOSAUR?   15

3 THE MESOZOIC ERA   26

4 DINOSAURS OF THE TRIASSIC PERIOD   34

5 DINOSAURS OF THE JURASSIC PERIOD   38

6 DINOSAURS OF THE EARLY CRETACEOUS PERIOD   45

7 DINOSAURS OF THE LATE CRETACEOUS PERIOD   50

8 FLYING AND SWIMMING REPTILES   61

9 THE GREAT DYING   67

10 MODERN-DAY DINOSAURS   73

   Glossary   78

The author wishes to thank the following dinosaur experts who read the manuscript and made valuable corrections and suggestions: David B. Weishampel, Assistant Professor, Department of Cell Biology and Anatomy, Johns Hopkins University School of Medicine; Jeannine Holdiman, Supervisor of School Programs, Maryland Science Center; Lynne Thornton, Public Relations Officer, and Sid Andrews, Head of Education Services, Tyrrell Museum of Palaeontology.

1

DINOSAUR BONES

Dragon bones

Long ago, someone discovered gigantic bones sticking out of a rock cliff. No one knew what kind of bones they were. The skull looked like it belonged to an enormous lizard with sharp teeth. Some people called them dragon bones and chopped them up to use in magic potions. But the truth was even more fantastic than the dragons they had suspected.

Later, in the 19th century, when huge skeletons were discovered in gravel quarries, the scientists of the day studied them. They realized that these were very old bones belonging to creatures that no longer inhabited the earth. These lizardlike animals must have been tremendous, and, by the look of their huge, dagger-sharp teeth, very dangerous. They called them "dinosaurs," from the Greek words "deinos," meaning terrible, and "sauros," meaning lizard.

For 140 million years (sixty million years before the first human appeared) dinosaurs dominated the earth. In that long reign, many types of dinosaurs appeared, developed, then disappeared to be replaced by other types. As the land, plants and climate changed on our planet, the dinosaurs changed too. Then suddenly, sixty-five million years ago, all the dinosaurs died.

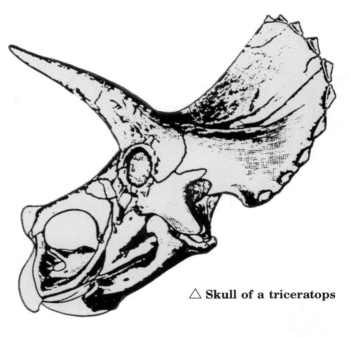

△ **Skull of a triceratops**

The mystery

Today we are left with many questions. Where did dinosaurs come from? What did they look like? What was their world like? Did they live in groups? Did they take care of their young? How did they adapt to the many environmental changes? And, most curious of all, what was it that caused all the dinosaurs to die?

A good mystery always attracts lots of detectives. In the case of dinosaurs, these detectives are called "paleontologists." Like detectives, they search for clues, examine the evidence and try

5

to put the pieces of the puzzle together. Unfortunately, most of the pieces of the dinosaur puzzle are missing.

The evidence

What clues could possibly last for more than sixty million years? The answer is fossils. Under certain special conditions, the remains of a plant or animal can be preserved for hundreds of millions of years!

Imagine that it is 140 million years ago. A young, long-necked apatosaur who has wandered away from its herd stands by the bank of a wide, meandering river nibbling the topmost leaves of a tree. As it browses, the eyes scan the horizon for any sign of danger. It doesn't see the pair of ferocious and hungry allosaurs behind the nearby trees, waiting to ambush the unsuspecting plant-eater.

The female allosaur sees its chance and comes charging, its huge jaws agape and lined with enormous knife-like teeth. It lunges, its powerful jaws clamping shut on the flesh behind the apatosaur's neck. But the mighty force of the attack pushes both dinosaurs into the river. The apatosaur lashes its whiplike tail at the fearsome predator, but the struggle is useless. The thirty-ton (27.2 t) apatosaur heaves and collapses on the allosaur and the two sink and drown beneath the river's waters.

The soft parts of the two dinosaur bodies, the skin and the muscles, decay quickly. The skeletons that are left are rapidly buried by river silt and mud. Gradually, over many thousands of years, the silt, or sediment, hardens into rock and is covered by many more layers of mud and silt, each eventually hardening into another layer, or strata, of rock.

The dinosaur bones of the apatosaur and allosaur now lie beneath many layers of sedimentary rock. If you could

cut away a portion of the earth, you would see these strata, stacked up like the layers of a cake, each representing millions of years in the earth's past. But why haven't the bones been crushed by the weight of the rock above?

While the earth's crust was stacking up, water was seeping down. When it reached the bones, it soaked into every tiny opening, bringing with it minerals. As the bones dissolved, each molecule was replaced by a molecule of mineral. What remains is an exact replica of the bone, only now it is made of stone—a fossil!

Of course many, many dinosaurs died and were not fossilized. They were eaten by predators or scavengers and their bones decayed. The skeletons that paleontologists find belong to a small percentage of all the dinosaurs that walked the earth.

Besides fossilized bones, dinosaur detectives look for what are called "trace fossils," such as footprints, eggs, even droppings (coprolites) which can reveal what the dinosaur ate.

Paleontologists have dug up the fossilized remains of more than 300 kinds of dinosaurs. How did they know where to look?

◁ **Two allosaurs ambush an apatosaur.**

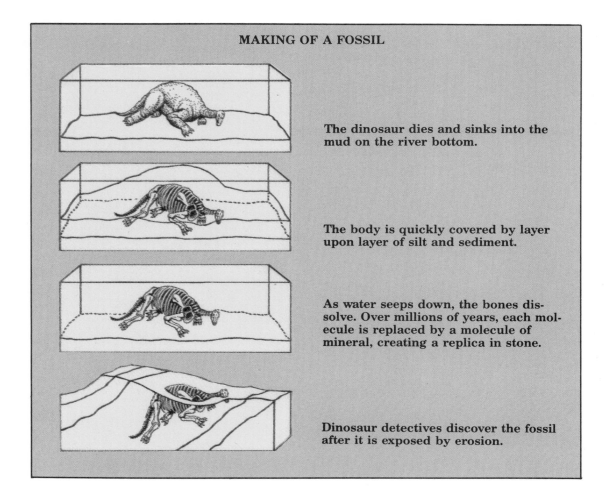

MAKING OF A FOSSIL

The dinosaur dies and sinks into the mud on the river bottom.

The body is quickly covered by layer upon layer of silt and sediment.

As water seeps down, the bones dissolve. Over millions of years, each molecule is replaced by a molecule of mineral, creating a replica in stone.

Dinosaur detectives discover the fossil after it is exposed by erosion.

The search for clues

Fossils are formed in sedimentary rock like sandstone and limestone. Deeper rock layers were formed before the ones above it. By examining the layers where dinosaur remains have been found before, paleontologists have determined in which layers they should be looking.

The search is for fossil-bearing layers that have been exposed by cliffs, river banks, road cuts or quarries. A fresh exposure is best but often an old cliff face, worn away by wind and rain, will suddenly reveal a long-kept secret.

Let's imagine that a fossil-seeking team discovers the skeletons of the allosaur and the apatosaur. As any good detective knows, the first order of business is to photograph the find in order to record its position. It may look like a big jumble of bones, but the bones' arrangement in the rock could be an important clue later on in the investigation. After this bone bed blueprint is made, the excavators begin their work. Using picks and chisels, hammers and brushes, even jack hammers and earth movers if the skeletons are quite large, they carefully cut from the cliff the piece of rock containing the fossils. The packers wrap the rock in paper and then seal it in plaster of Paris to prevent any damage during transport to the museum laboratory.

At the laboratory, the plaster is removed. Now begins the painstaking work of separating the fossils from the sedimentary rock. Paleontologists use ultrasonic probes, tiny chisels, vibrating needles, diamond cutting wheels, wire brushes and acid solutions to carefully clean the fossils. Then the bones are sorted, photographed, measured and labeled. If the bones will be used to reconstruct the dinosaur, perhaps for use in a museum, fiberglass casts are made of each bone. These lightweight casts can be more easily assembled and supported than the heavy fossils themselves. Extra casts of a skeleton are often made to trade to other museums. The fragile, original fossils are kept for further study.

The discoveries

The search for dinosaur remains has revealed some fantastic dinosaur bone beds. During the late 19th century, two American fossil hunters, Othniel Charles Marsh and Edward Drinker Cope, had a race to see who could discover the most dinosaur skeletons. Excavating rock formations in Colorado and Wyoming, these two rivals filled American museums with the remains of at least 136 new kinds of dinosaurs. Professor Marsh and his team of fossil hunters added eighty names to the new species list, including Diplodocus, Allosaurus, Stegosaurus and Triceratops, while Mr. Cope and

Edward Drinker Cope

Othniel Charles Marsh

9

his crew discovered fifty-six new kinds of dinosaurs, including Monoclonius and Coelophysis.

A later expedition, in 1898, from the American Museum of Natural History to Wyoming, resulted in the discovery of Bone Cabin Quarry. Paleontologists found dinosaur bones littering the ground there. In fact, the site got its name because the bones were so abundant that a shepherd had used them to build himself a small shelter. In the first year of excavation the fossil hunters at Bone Cabin Quarry shipped 60,000 pounds (27,216 kg) of dinosaur bones back to the museum!

An area that has yielded great dinosaur discoveries since the turn of the century is the Red Deer River in Alberta, Canada. The river has cut a deep path through the layers of rock. Dinosaur hunters built barges and floated

10

◁ **Mamenchisaurus had the longest neck of any known dinosaur.**

Asia has been the scene of the latest dinosaur rush. In fact, one quarter of all the known dinosaurs were discovered in Asia. An especially rich area for "dragon bones" is Sichuan province in the People's Republic of China where hundreds of skeletons have been unearthed, including the remains of Mamenchisaurus, a seventy-two-foot-long (21.9m) plant-eater with perhaps the longest neck of any dinosaur—thirty-three feet (10m)!

On the Gobi Desert in Mongolia, dinosaur bone beds have yielded the remains of many protoceratops, their nests and eggs. Scientists believe that these dinosaurs nested in colonies. Joint Soviet-Mongolian and Soviet-Polish expeditions have unearthed several skeletons of meat-eaters like Oviraptor (the "egg thief"), plus an especially chilling find—a pair of six-foot-long (1.8m) arms with enormous clawed hands. Deinocheirus ("terrible hand") was the name given to the dinosaur that used these monstrous arms and claws. Judging from the size of the bones, it may have been the biggest predator to ever walk the earth!

Recent South American fossil finds by José Bonaparte and his team include Saltasaurus, an armored dinosaur with two kinds of bony plates embedded in its skin, Lagosuchus ("rabbit crocodile"), perhaps one of the very earliest dinosaurs, and Mussaurus ("mouse lizard"), a baby dinosaur so small that you could hold it in your hand.

In Australia, hundreds of fossilized dinosaur footprints have been found. Is it possible that dinosaurs migrated along certain paths like many herd animals do today? Paleontologists are also studying the bones of a colossal dinosaur called the Hughenden sauropod.

down the river, keeping a sharp eye on the steep cliffs above. Expedition after expedition piled barges high with dinosaur bones, many from hadrosaurs, or "duckbill" dinosaurs. Today at the Red Deer River paleontologists are finding the bones from herds of centrosaurs, horned dinosaurs that roamed the western coastal plains.

Dinosaur National Monument, located in Utah, is a site so rich in dinosaur fossils that it has become a permanent museum where excavation work still goes on.

Of course, North America is not the only place where great dinosaur fossil discoveries have been made. Dinosaur bones have been found on every continent on earth, including Antarctica.

△ **Dinosaur bones are uncovered at Dinosaur National Monument in Utah.**

Other huge sauropods, such as eighty-ton (72.5 t) Brachiosaurus, have been unearthed in Africa, where bone beds have yielded enormous numbers of fossils. From one site alone, at the mouth of an African river, 250 tons (226.8 t) of dinosaur bones were found.

Europe's best-known bone bed was in Belgium. Coal miners there discovered the skeletons of thirty-nine iguanodons that had fallen to their deaths into a ravine.

Examining the evidence

What can paleontologists learn from studying the fossilized bones, skulls, teeth and claws of dinosaurs? By looking at all the evidence, they are able to guess what an individual dinosaur looked like. How big was it? Did it walk on two feet or four? Besides describing the size, weight and posture from the fossilized dinosaur pieces, the detectives ask: Were its teeth for grinding plants or tearing flesh? Do marks on the bones indicate large muscles?

How fast could it run? How did it move its jaw? What were its feet like? How many fingers did it have? From the shape of the skull, what did its head look like?

Fossil hunters rarely find a whole skeleton. Usually, many of the bones are missing. To guess what the missing bones may have looked like, scientists sometimes look at the skeletons of living reptiles that may resemble the long extinct one.

The habits of living animals can also shed light on dinosaur behavior. Suppose detectives find a dinosaur tooth that resembles the tooth of a living creature that can be observed first-hand. Seeing what the animal eats and how it chews its food can offer clues to the dinosaur's diet.

Teeth are the most commonly preserved part of a dinosaur. They are also the best clues to whether the dinosaur found is a plant-eater or a meat-eater. For example, if we look at the teeth of an allosaur, we can guess that it was probably a meat-eater. Its teeth are long, sharp and serrated, ideal for stab-

▽ **A paleontologist uses a small chisel to separate fossil from sedimentary rock.**

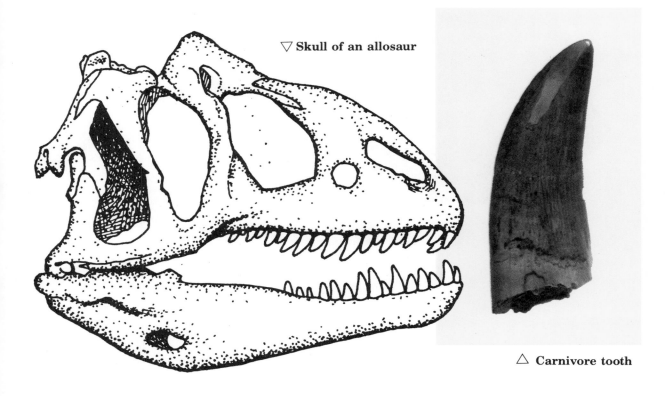

▽ Skull of an allosaur

△ Carnivore tooth

bing and tearing flesh.

The jaw of another dinosaur, an apatosaur, contains short, peglike teeth near the front that were probably used to pull the leaves from branches. Inside the ribcage, large smooth stones, called "gastroliths," were found. Paleontologists think that the giant plant-eaters swallowed stones to help them digest tough plant matter.

Bumps, crests and worn spots on the bones can show where muscles were attached. These powerful muscles worked to help the heavy creatures walk, run and leap. The evidence shows that Allosaurus walked on two legs and needed powerful leg muscles to move quickly and support its heavy frame. The weight of its massive skull and snapping jaw also required strong muscles.

The skull of Apatosaurus has large eyesockets, spaced far apart but aimed forward, suggesting keen eyesight. Apatosaurus's long neck probably also helped it spot approaching predators.

It is evident from the bones of this apatosaur that it had been attacked by an allosaur. Scrapes on the bones match the spacing of the allosaur's teeth. The bite mark is unmistakable.

Besides looking at the bones themselves, paleontologists can learn something about the dinosaurs' environment by studying other fossils in the same rock layers as the dinosaurs. Fossil impressions of ferns and conifers give a key to the diet of plant-eating dinosaurs like Apatosaurus. Fossilized insects, lizards, amphibians and mammals can tell about who shared the dinosaurs' world and who provided a food

△ **Fossilized leaf**

source for many of the smaller meat-eaters.

A good detective keeps an open mind and seeks out the truth, even when the answers keep changing. Recently, there have been discoveries that have challenged old ideas about what dinosaurs were like. These new ideas have sent paleontologists back to the evidence for a fresh look. For instance, for many years scientists believed that dinosaurs were sluggish creatures that lumbered around through jungles and swamps. Today there is evidence that many dinosaurs were fast and agile, with keen senses. They may have been warm-blooded. Certainly some kinds traveled in grazing herds, others in hunting packs. There is also evidence that some dinosaur parents took care of their young.

Every detective wishes he or she had a magic mirror and could see the whole picture instead of merely pieces of the puzzle. There are some answers that we cannot easily learn from sixty-five million-year-old clues. For instance, were dinosaurs brightly colored like many modern-day reptiles? Did some of them have feathers? How fast did a dinosaur grow and what was its lifespan? What did a dinosaur sound like? Did it hoot, honk, bellow or whimper?

It seems that the mysteries surrounding the dinosaurs may never be solved, but the search for clues is as exciting as any treasure hunt!

2

WHAT IS A DINOSAUR?

Dinosaur family tree

Dinosaurs were land animals. They did not swim or fly. But their ancestors and relatives did. Where did dinosaurs come from and how did they fit in with other animals in their world?

In order to understand the similarities and differences between dinosaurs and other animals, scientists gave dinosaurs a place in a classifying system that includes every animal we know about that ever lived on this planet. To decide in which group a living animal belongs, scientists look at the way the animal behaves, how its body works and how it has babies. Of course, with dinosaurs and other extinct animals this isn't possible. Bones, eggs and footprints are all they have to go on.

After studying the evidence they had, scientists placed dinosaurs in the Reptilia class along with snakes and lizards, and divided dinosaurs into two orders: Ornithischia ("bird hips") and Saurichia ("reptile hips") according to the shape of their pelvis bones. Both these orders of dinosaurs descended from an ancestor group called the Thecodontia (teeth-in-sockets), named because these particular reptiles had developed teeth that sat deep in the sockets in the jawbone.

Thecodonts were meat-eating reptiles that lived 225 million years ago. They had strong hind legs and short forelegs. Instead of sprawling, they drew their elbows and knees in close to their bodies and lifted their bellies from the ground when they walked. Strong hind legs allowed them to lift their chests and forelegs off the ground and sprint. Thecodonts may have had the edge over other reptiles because their improved posture gave them greater running speed for catching prey. Other meat-eating reptile groups

▽ **Dinosaur footprint**

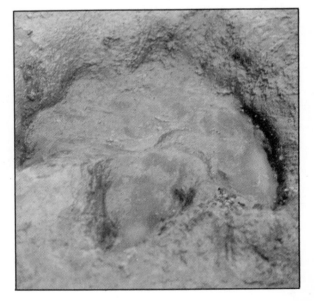

15

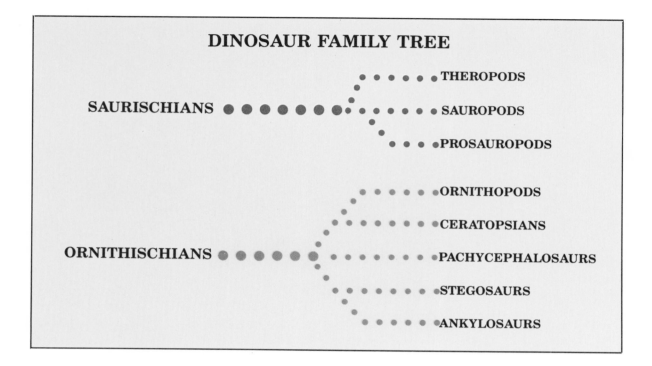

DINOSAUR FAMILY TREE

SAURISCHIANS
- THEROPODS
- SAUROPODS
- PROSAUROPODS

ORNITHISCHIANS
- ORNITHOPODS
- CERATOPSIANS
- PACHYCEPHALOSAURS
- STEGOSAURS
- ANKYLOSAURS

couldn't compete and were finally crowded out.

About 215 million years ago, a line of thecodonts gave rise to the first dinosaurs. These small creatures could run on their back legs for long distances with their long tails held out to balance the weight of their torsos. Other animals that descended from the thecodonts were crocodiles and pterosaurs (flying reptiles), distant cousins of the dinosaurs.

Saurichians

Dinosaurs in the saurischian order may have had the same kind of pelvis bone, but they were as different from each other as dogs are from horses and hamsters. Within this order are three kinds of dinosaurs: theropods, prosauropods and sauropods.

Theropods are divided into large

carnosaurs, like Allosaurus and the huge meat-eater Tyrannosaurus, and the smaller meat-eating coelurosaurs, such as Compsognathus and Deinonychus. The little coelurosaurs developed into large-brained creatures with keen senses—the most highly developed reptiles of all time. Prosauropods were the first plant-eating dinosaurs and ancestors of the gigantic sauropods, such as the eighty-foot-long (24 m) Apatosaurus.

Ornithischians

The ornithischian ("bird-hipped") order of dinosaurs has five different groups, all plant-eaters:

1. ornithopods, such as spikythumbed Iguanodon and the duckbills
2. ceratopsians, horned dinosaurs, such as Triceratops and Centrosaurus
3. pachycephalosaurs, boneheads

16

who had ten-inch-thick (25 m) bone in their skulls

4. stegosaurs, plated dinosaurs

5. ankylosaurs, armored dinosaurs

Some paleontologists argue that there are so many differences between dinosaurs and other reptiles that they ought to be put in their own class called the Dinosauria. This class, they propose, would include the orders Saurischia, Ornithischia and Aves (birds!).

Dinosaur family life

In 1978, fossil hunters Jack Horner and Robert Makela made a famous discovery in Montana. They found a bowl-shaped mud nest, six feet (1.8 m) across and three feet (91 cm) deep. In the nest were fifteen duckbill hatchlings! It is rare to find dinosaur nests, fossilized eggs or babies. The driest, safest places for nests did not provide the best conditions for fossilizing. What made Horner and Makela's find especially exciting was that the hatchlings in the nest were not newborns. Their teeth showed wear from chewing leaves and berries. Parent duckbills had been bringing the babies food until they were old enough to leave the nest and take care of themselves.

Horner and Makela have returned to the nesting site year after year and each season they uncover more nests. Altogether they have found over 200 nests, some with eggs still containing embryos, some with hatchlings and trampled bits of eggshell, and some with rather large dinosaur youngsters. The remains of duckbill adults were found near the nests. Horner and Makela named this new species of dinosaur Maiasaura, or "good mother lizard."

Eighty million years ago at the site, when a mother maiasaura dug her nest and laid her eggs, she was probably on an island or peninsula in a shallow lake protected somewhat from predators. Each year the adult maiasauras made the journey from the green, wet forests of the lowlands up to this hilly, drier region to a common nesting

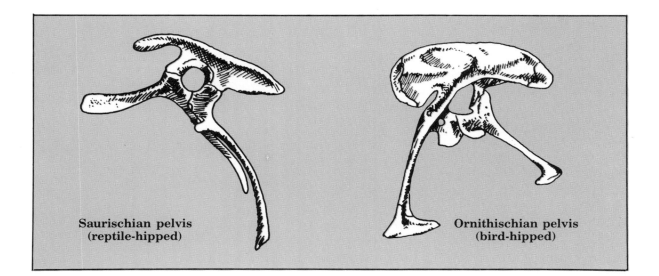

Saurischian pelvis
(reptile-hipped)

Ornithischian pelvis
(bird-hipped)

ground. Here the mothers dug their nests twenty-four feet (7.3 m) apart, about the length of an adult maiasaura. Each mother laid about twenty softball-sized eggs in a circle, then covered them with leaves and twigs.

Nesting together had its advantages. When one mother was away getting food, other mothers could keep an eye out for sharp-toothed coelurosaurs who might be waiting for a chance to raid the nests for a meal of eggs.

Finally, when it was time, little peeping thirteen-inch-long (33 cm) dinosaurs pecked out of the eggs. The mother maiasaura uncovered the nest. Like hungry baby birds, they cheeped and peeped, mouths open wide until the mother returned with a mouthful of seeds and berries which it had already chewed for them.

The babies stayed and grew in the nest until they were old enough to follow their mother to the lake's edge to feed on berries themselves. They learned where to look for food and how to avoid danger. At night they returned to the nest to sleep.

When the young were old enough to make the trip, the maiasaura families gathered together in one huge herd to journey back to the lowlands where food was plentiful. Hundreds of dinosaurs made the month-long trip, traveling over 100 miles (161 km) back to the coast of the inland sea.

Other kinds of dinosaurs cared for and protected their young. Footprints of a herd of apatosaurs in Como Bluff, Wyoming show that adults walked on the outside of the group, while the youngsters walked in the middle where they were safer from predators. This same pattern was followed by ceratopsians. When threatened by large carnosaurs, triceratops adults formed a ring around their young and faced the enemy with horns ready.

Living in herds was important protection for plant-eating dinosaurs of all ages. To find food, they had to be constantly on the move, wandering over long distances in unfamiliar territory. Moving in groups may have made them more obvious prey, but there was safety in numbers. There were more eyes to keep a lookout for danger. A danger signal could trigger a stampede, leaving predators in the dust trying to pick out a victim. A single meat-eater was less likely to face a half-dozen plant-eaters with defensive weapons like horns or lashing tails.

But there was more to a herd than numbers. A herd was a family group of parents, children, aunts, uncles and cousins. The strongest males were the

leaders of the herd. They kept an eye out for danger and led the others in retreat or battle. It was their job to face the enemy when the herd was cornered. The females preferred them as mates.

In order to keep their jobs, these leaders needed to prove that they were the strongest. Other males in the herd challenged them to contests. Some dinosaurs, like the pachycephalosaurs (boneheads) had butting contests, running into each other and crashing head-on like bighorn sheep. Others, like Triceratops, locked horns and pushed to test strength.

Hadrosaurs and other dinosaurs unequipped to fight competed for leadership and mates by showing off. They developed oddly shaped and perhaps brightly colored crests on the tops of their heads. Males whose crests made them look bigger and more attractive

◁ **Maiasaura nesting ground**

than their rivals won more mates and leadership in the herd.

But herds were not entirely safe. Meat-eating hunters may have had strategies of their own. It is likely that they formed hunting packs and cooperated in attacking prey. Even small predators could bring down large game if they worked together. Perhaps the meat-eating dinosaurs hunted like today's lions of the African plain that hide behind trees or hills, their skin color blending in with the background so they aren't easily spotted. When a herd of plant-eaters was spread out feeding, the hunters slowly closed in on a weak or young one farthest from the group. All at once they would attack, sending the rest of the herd into confusion. While they killed their victim, the rest of the herd ran away.

You can bet that the kill was not shared equally among the hunters. In this group, too, there were probably leaders feared by their rivals who took the "lion's share" of the food. Perhaps hunting packs were territorial, as wolf packs are today. Packs may have stayed within their borders when there was enough food passing through or plundered neighboring pack's territory when food was more scarce. Perhaps they followed the herds of plant-eaters when they came together in massive numbers for seasonal migrations.

Seasonal migrations of dinosaur herds were common. Just like birds who fly south to avoid the winter cold and find food in the warmer regions, dinosaurs followed the rains north and south to feed upon young tender shoots.

Dinosaur detective Phil Currie believes that in North America, during the last part of the age of the dinosaurs, small herds joined together in huge herds every year and headed north to the Arctic. Of course, the Arctic was not nearly as cold as it is now. It was a placed to find plants to eat when the dry season farther south caused plant life to wither. Currie hopes to find evidence of the same dinosaur herds from Alberta, Canada, farther north near the Arctic Circle. A recent dinosaur find in Alaska could be what he is looking for!

Dinosaur predators depended on speed, strength, agility, sharp teeth and claws and hunting cooperation to catch their food. To avoid predators, plant-eaters developed defensive weapons like horns and spiked thumbs and tails, enormous size, armor, speed, keen senses and herd protection.

Both predators and prey probably depended on camouflage. Blending into the surroundings gave hunters the edge of a surprise attack and gave prey a chance to escape unseen. If we look at living animals and their environments we see that forest dwellers are often dappled brown or green. A spotted fawn can sit motionless in a thicket and never be noticed. On more open ground, contrasting stripes disguise the shape of an animal. Herds of zebras and antelope can disappear at a distance. We can only guess at dinosaur coloring, but animals today may be following the dinosaur pattern for camouflage.

Cold-blooded or warm-blooded?

Its been 150 years since dinosaurs were named "terrible lizards." Because dinosaurs were reptilian in some ways, scientists assumed that they were like living reptiles in all ways. They were pictured as slow, sluggish creatures who walked like lizards, elbows pointing out and bellies slung low. They

▽ **Some scientists think that the active hunter, Deinonychus, had to be warm-blooded.**

lived solitary lives, wandering the tropical swamps, eating aquatic plants or preying on slow, unwary individuals. Of course, it was believed that just like living reptiles, all dinosaurs were cold-blooded.

In the past twenty years, dinosaur detectives have questioned this picture of the dinosaurs. Now they have thrown it out altogether. A new look at the evidence shows that dinosaurs did not fit the old idea of them as lizardlike.

One dinosaur that turned the old ideas around was Deinonychus, a five-foot-tall (1.5 m) meat-eater with a slashing claw on its foot. The more paleontologist John Ostrom studied the bones of the newly-discovered Deinonychus, the more puzzled he became. In order to kill with his foot claw, Deinonychus must have leaped, pounced and stood on one foot while kicking with the other. A cold-blooded reptile doesn't have the energy required to do those things. Ostrom began to wonder whether Deinonychus may have been warm-blooded.

Cold-blooded animals, like snakes

21

and lizards, are called ectotherms. Ecto means "outside" and therm means "heat." A cold-blooded animal has no inside way to control its body temperature. It has to depend on the warmth of the sun to heat up its body and allow any activity. That is why a snake must bask in the sun each morning before it can move about to hunt for food. Most of a reptile's day is spent motionless, waiting for enough heat to be active for a short time. If the sun gets too hot, an ectotherm must seek the shade or burrow in the ground to cool its body or it will die.

Mammals and birds are warm-blooded animals, or endotherms; endo means "inside." They have an inside way to control body temperature. An endotherm's body engine works hard to keep its body the right temperature all the time, whether the sun is shining or not. Hair and feathers help to hold in body heat. When the sun is too hot, an endotherm can cool off by sweating or panting. Endotherms are always ready for action and can stay active all day.

The source of heat inside an endotherm's body is high metabolism. That means the body machine burns more fuel to keep the animal warm and active. An endotherm must eat a lot more food than an ectotherm. For instance, a lion eats its weight in food every seven to ten days. An ectotherm, like a Komodo dragon, a ten-foot-long (3 m) meat-eating reptile, eats its weight in food every sixty days!

There is no way to get direct evidence to prove that dinosaurs were endotherms or ectotherms. We can't put a thermometer under a dinosaur's tongue and take its temperature! Detectives have only bones and footprints to study. But there are clues. . .

On the warm side

Clue #1. Unlike their relatives the crocodiles, who can only live in warm areas nearest to the equator, dinosaurs once roamed near the Arctic Circle. They must have had internal heating systems to withstand the big changes in temperature.

Clue #2. Most dinosaurs had erect posture, that is their legs were directly under their bodies. No living reptiles have erect posture. All living animals with erect posture are endotherms.

Clue #3. Living reptiles have two-chambered hearts and low blood pressure. But in a Brachiosaurus, for example, the distance between the heart and the brain was nearly twenty feet (6 m)! The Brachiosaurus's heart had to pump the blood up that distance to its brain. Many would argue that it is not possible for a two-chambered heart to pump blood up that high. The job would require a four-chambered heart and high blood pressure—both signs of a warm-blooded creature.

Clue #4. Small hunters such as Compsognathus were swift and agile, running on two legs with stiffened tails held out for balance. "Ostrich dinosaurs" were built for speed. Strong muscles and hip and ankle construction show that these creatures could reach speeds of fifty miles (80 km) per hour. No living reptiles could have managed the speed of an ostrich dinosaur or have kept up the activity level for as long as Compsognathus.

Clue #5. When dinosaur bone is put under the microscope, it shows a network of tiny holes or canals where blood vessels used to pass through the bone. Mammal and bird bones have this same network of holes. Reptilian bones show only a few holes.

Clue #6. Many dinosaurs were huge, longer than a playground and taller than an apartment building. But how big were they when they hatched out of their eggs? If we look at one kind of thirty-five-foot (10.6 m) dinosaur that has been found with newly hatched and older babies, we find that the babies were thirteen inches long (33 cm) when they hatched. By the end of the first year, the babies were ten feet long (3 m). They grew nine feet (2.7 m) in one year!

Living reptiles do not grow quickly. A crocodile grows about a foot a year. An ostrich baby, an endotherm, grows much more quickly, as much as five feet (1.5 m) in one year.

Clue #7. Endotherms must eat often and digest food quickly. Their heat-producing bodies need constant refueling. Teeth that chew help break

▷ A brachiosaur's heart had to pump blood nearly twenty feet (6 m) to its brain.

down food and provide a head start on the digestion process.

Several families of dinosaurs had very special teeth. These cutting and grinding teeth helped break down hard-to-digest leaves and seeds.

Reptiles (ectotherms) do not chew. They eat infrequently and don't need to process the food quickly for fast energy.

Clue #8. If meat-eating dinosaurs were endothermic and had to hunt more often than reptiles, there would have to be enough prey to let them survive.

When paleontologist Robert Bakker counted the fossilized remains from one period in the age of the dinosaurs, he found that overall, hunters made up three percent of the whole dinosaur population. That's one meat-eating Tyrannosaurus, for instance, for every thirty plant-eating duckbills, ceratopsians or ankylosaurs. The population numbers suggest that meat-eating dinosaurs were endothermic predators.

But this is all indirect evidence. It can't be proved. Some dinosaur experts argue that there are big holes in the warm-blooded theory.

On the cold side

Clue #1. The climate in the world during the Mesozoic Era, when the dinosaurs lived, was mild. Seasonal temperature did not vary much, so the creatures did not have to make any major adjustments for cold winters or hot summers.

Clue #2. A microscopic look at some ectothermic crocodile bones shows the same network of vessel canals as do dinosaur, mammal and bird bones. Also, some mammal bones resemble the cross section of reptile bones.

Clue #3. If all dinosaurs were endothermic, then why did some, like Stegosaurus and Spinosaurus, develop systems of plates and sails to collect heat from the sun and radiate heat to

◁ **Did an endothermic stegosaur need plates to regulate its body temperature?**

cool off? (Warm-blooded dinosaur supporters point out that many warm-blooded animals today, such as African elephants, have large ears to dissipate heat.)

Clue #4. Counting the fossil population is not the same as counting the actual dinosaur population. Certain dinosaurs might have had lifestyles that made them more likely to be fossilized. Perhaps they lived near a shallow lake on a flood plain where bodies might be covered in mud and silt to be preserved. Other dinosaurs may have lived in the uplands where their bodies did not have the same chance to be quickly covered and preserved.

Fossil collectors, especially from the great fossil rush at the turn of the century, collected whole skeletons that they knew would be bought by museums. They often ignored pieces of skeletons that might not be as saleable. So the collected fossils might not even reflect the real fossil population.

Clue #5. If dinosaurs were endothermic, why did they grow so large? If a huge sauropod, such as Apatosaurus or Brachiosaurus, was endothermic, it would have had to eat a ton of food a day! There aren't enough hours in a day for that small mouth to take in so much food.

The fact is, a large body holds on to heat longer. The bulk of a big ectothermic dinosaur could stabilize its body temperature. This would leave it free to move at a slow but steady pace.

But what about small, very active dinosaurs like Ornitholestes, a forty-pound (18 kg) meat-eater? Body bulk did not regulate its body temperature.

New evidence, new theories, new questions. As the debate about cold-blooded and warm-blooded dinosaurs goes on, detectives stir up new interest in dinosaurs. We want to learn more details about how they lived. Were there special leaders in a triceratops herd? How did little Compsognathus survive? Was a tyrannosaur cunning and smart? Did Apatosaurus really have live babies? Exactly what plants did plated Stegosaurus nibble with its small mouth? Did allosaur parents take care of their meat-eating young?

Of course, there are bigger questions, too. What was the world like when the dinosaurs lived here? How did land, water, climate and plants change in 140 million years? How did dinosaurs change to survive?

3

THE MESOZOIC ERA

It is very difficult for our minds to grasp how long ago the dinosaurs lived. This is because people think in terms of lifetimes—seventy or eighty years. We are able to picture how many years have passed since our grandparents were children. We can even count the years backwards to the Revolutionary War, or count the centuries back to the building of ancient cities. But nothing people have experienced gives them the scale they need to count the 200 million years backwards to the age of the dinosaurs!

After all, our written history began only 6,000 years ago. Our ancestors evolved a mere three to four million years ago. In the life of this four and a half billion-year-old planet, our existence has been a blink of an eye.

But the earth's hidden story is kept for us, written in the layer upon layer of rock, built up and worn down over millions of years. What we learn from rocks and fossils can make that enormously distant time come alive again.

To be able to imagine what the dinosaurs' world was like, we need to know more than how big a dinosaur was or how fast it could run. Scientists want to know about dinosaur ecology—how dinosaurs interacted with the animals and plants around them. What part did they play in the web of life 200 million years ago?

Preserved in the rock layers along

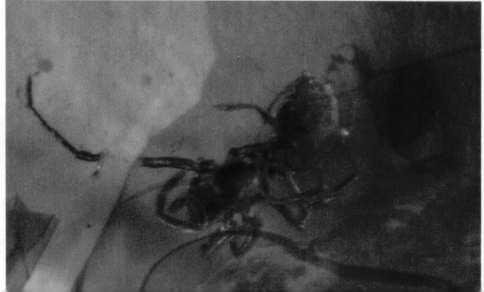

◁ A spider preserved in amber (fossilized tree sap).

with the remains of dinosaurs are also fossils of the plants, insects, mammals, amphibians and reptiles that shared the dinosaurs' world. The color of certain layers can reveal whether the climate was dry, wet or seasonal. Fossils of fish, mollusks and other water dwellers show where and when inland seas and lakes existed. This evidence helps dinosaur detectives put together a picture of the landscape and climate of what is called the Mesozoic Era, the age of the dinosaurs.

The Mesozoic Era began 225 million years ago and ended sixty-five million years ago, about the same time that the last dinosaur disappeared. In that time the face of the earth changed drastically: continents broke up, land sank and huge inland seas formed, climates changed, deserts grew and shrank, mountains were pushed up then worn down by water and wind. But, despite these upheavals throughout the Mesozoic, dinosaurs were the most successful creatures on earth.

Geologist have divided this era into three periods according to rock strata—the Triassic [try-ASS-ik], the Jurassic [jer-ASS-ik] and the Cretaceous [Kreh-TAY-shus] Periods.

The Triassic Period

The Triassic Period lasted about thirty-five million years, from the beginning of the Mesozoic Era until 190 million years ago. At the beginning of the Triassic Period, all the land on earth was in one huge mass, crowded together on one side of the globe. This supercontinent is called Pangaea [pan-JEE-uh], meaning "all earth." The climate throughout Pangaea was mild; there were no cold temperatures or oceans to keep animals from moving freely about the single continent.

Wide, slow-moving rivers wound through lush green forests of giant fern trees, horsetails, ginkgos and palm-like cycads with thick trunks. It was hot and humid, like Florida in the summertime. Daily thunderstorms filled the rivers, often causing flash floods that swept up great quantities of mud and silt and deposited them downstream. On higher ground, above the floodplains, grew conifers that resembled the Norfolk Island pines of today.

The interior of the continent, what is now Africa, was untouched by the rain that fell nearer to the coasts, so the land was dry desert.

It was during the middle of the Triassic that the first dinosaurs appeared. By the end of the period there were many species living on the floodplains, along the huge rivers and in the nearby upland forests. Meat-eating theropods, like Coelophysis and little Procompsognathus, ran through the undergrowth, pouncing on lizards that they held in their grasping claws. Herds of long-necked, plant-eating prosauropods like Plateosaurus roamed the forests, stopping often to munch on cycads and ferns.

Meanwhile, the first pterosaur (flying reptile) soared overhead. Early crocodiles inhabited the rivers, preying on animals that came to drink at the water's edge. Primitive shrew-like mammals hid in burrows all day and only ventured out at night to feed on insects.

During the Late Triassic, Pangaea broke in half. The two pieces gradually drifted apart and formed two land masses—Laurasia (what is now North America, Europe, Asia, Greenland and Iceland) and Gondwanaland (what is now South America, Africa, India, Australia and Antarctica). Worldwide climate grew seasonally warmer and drier.

Plants and animals gradually changed their habits, diet or body style to adapt to this environmental change, or they died out. Ferns, which could

▷ **Position of the continents during the Triassic Period, 200 million years ago.**

only spread by showering spores on wet soil, had to yield more ground to gymnosperms, plants whose seeds could wait until the rains came to sprout.

As the plants changed, the dinosaurs that fed on them changed too. They developed belly stones or chewing teeth to grind up the tough leaves of the gymnosperms. They also traveled in herds, following the rainy season. Meat-eating dinosaurs adapted their hunting habits to their prey.

Dinosaurs and mammals seem to have appeared about the same time during the Triassic. Why did reptilian dinosaurs develop and take over, growing in size, number and kinds while the primitive mammal remained a small insignificant ratlike creature during the entire Mesozoic Era?

One theory is that at the very end of the Triassic, earth's inhabitants had to cope with an unknown catastrophe, in addition to the hotter, drier climate. For some reason, the fossil record shows, there were many extinctions of plants and animals at the end of the Triassic. The ecological niches left empty by extinct species were quickly filled by the archosaurs (dinosaurs and crocodiles). No one knows why the mammals, who had an equal chance to fill those empty niches, didn't do so. But once the dinosaurs and crocodiles were established, the small mammals could not compete for food and habitats. It seems that archosaurs were simply the first ones to get a foot in the door!

The Jurassic Period

As the two supercontinents, Laurasia and Gondwanaland, drifted apart, the space between them became a huge sea. Rain fell on the deserts that had been deep in the heart of the continent. Earth movement caused land to sink and water rushed in to form shallow inland seas and lakes. Other land was pushed up to form mountains. The climate became warm and wet, just what tropical plants need to multiply and thrive.

Forests of tree ferns and ground ferns, pines, sequoias, ginkgos and cycads provided an abundant food supply for plant-eating dinosaurs. The forests were also an excellent habitat for many insects, such as flies, mosquitoes and ants, which were a source of food for the lizards and frogs, which in turn were an important part of a small meat-eating dinosaur's diet. More forest meant more food for all. With a bigger food supply, dinosaurs grew not only in numbers and variety, but also grew to be giants!

The long-necked sauropods, such as Apatosaurus and Brachiosaurus, could

◁ Coelophysis, a small Triassic meat-eater, corners its prey, a mammal.

nibble the topmost leaves of the trees. The biggest of all, Ultrasaurus, probably managed to touch branches sixty feet (18 m) off the ground. Herds of these enormous creatures thundered through the forests, stripping a broad path of vegetation. In these newly-made open areas, the smaller theropods like Compsognathus and Ornitholestes hunted their game of lizards, insects and possibly birds.

Preying on the giant sauropods were huge carnosaurs such as thirty-foot-long (9 m) Allosaurus. Ornithopods, such as Camptosaurus, munched on lower tree branches, while plated Stegosaurus cropped the ground plants.

As the Jurassic came to an end 135 million years ago, the continents continued to pull apart. A sea opened up between South America and Africa. Land that had been covered by the inland seas rose again to become swamps, forests and broad river floodplains.

It is believed that at the end of the Jurassic, a calamity befell the earth, a drastic change that caused many species of animals and plants to die out, just as at the end of the Triassic. Although some sauropods survived into the Cretaceous Period, the golden age of the giant treetop-eaters was over.

The Cretaceous Period

It may sound as if the huge land masses were moving about the planet

▽ **Position of the continents during the Jurassic Period, 150 million years ago.**

like great ocean liners. In reality, during the Mesozoic Era the continents moved only an inch or so every year. They are moving at that same rate today!

In the Cretaceous Period, which lasted seventy million years, Gondwanaland split apart. Africa broke off while Australia, India and Antarctica drifted to the southeast. Eventually India separated from the other land mass and floated northeast toward Asia. Laurasia stayed in one piece but in the late Cretaceous an inland sea 1,000 miles (1,609 km) wide divided it into a western and eastern part.

The climate during the Cretaceous became more distinctly seasonal—rainy and steamy or hot and dry. Perhaps it was the change in climate that caused something truly wonderful to

▽ **A stegosaur prepares to defend itself against an attacking allosaur.**

▷ **A young parasaurolophus finds refuge from a hungry tyrannosaur.**

appear for the first time, something we admire and enjoy today—flowers!

The great forests that stretched between the inland seas now included magnolias, dogwoods, oaks, hickories, maples, willows, honeysuckle, holly, poplars and walnut trees as well as palms and evergreens. New types of trees and plants meant new kinds of dinosaurs to feed on them. Hadrosaurs (duckbills with special chewing teeth), ankylosaurs, ceratopsians and pachycephalosaurus all browsed in the Cretaceous forests on lower branches and ground plants. Predators, such as Tyrannosaurus, grew enormous feeding on the abundance of herd dinosaurs and, by thinning the herds, kept the plant-eaters from overthinning the forests.

Sharing the forest with dinosaurs were snakes, lizards, salamanders, frogs, turtles, snails, opossumlike and shrewlike mammals and over 1,000 species of insects.

Birds, bees and butterflies took to the air in the Cretaceous, as did the biggest animal ever to fly, Quetzalcoatlus, a flying reptile with a forty-foot (12 m) wingspan. In the

△ The position of the continents during the Late Cretaceous Period, seventy million years ago.

swamps, huge crocodiles floated among the water lilies and cattails. Enormous creatures inhabited the inland seas, such as plesiosaurs and mosasaurs.

But the most numerous animals of the time were plant-eating dinosaurs. Paleontologist Robert Bakker has said that plant-eating dinosaurs of the Cretaceous not only adapted to eating flowering plants—they invented them!

The ground browsers ate low shrubs and seedlings. They cropped plants right down to the bare earth. It was in these bare spots that early flowering plants got their foothold in the forest. Conifers could spread their seed over the bare soil but they grew slowly. Angiosperms (flowering plants), however, distributed their seeds over these bare spots, and the seeds germinated and grew quickly. Their flowers bloomed and went to seed before the herds of plant munchers could return and eat the blossoms. In this way the flowering plants had opportunities to spread throughout forests where conifers once dominated. Perhaps without the help of the dinosaurs creating bare spots in the Cretaceous forest, we would not have the enormous variety of flowering plants that grow in every part of the world today.

33

4

DINOSAURS OF THE TRIASSIC PERIOD

Procompsognathus — "before pretty jaw"

Procompsognathus [pro-komp-so-NAY-thus], like Coelophysis, was a coelurosaur, the earliest group of dinosaurs. It, too, was a small, active meateater with hollow bones and birdlike feet. It stood eleven and one-half inches (29 cm) tall and four feet (1.2 m) long from its snout to the tip of its very long tail. Procompsognathus ran on its toes, leaning forward to grab insects and small mammals in its four-fingered hands.

Much of what paleontologists know about the way Procompsognathus walked and ran is from footprint clues. An "ichnologist" is a special kind of paleontologist who studies fossilized footprints. By examining footprints, an ichnologist can tell whether a dinosaur walked on two feet or four, how heavy it was, how fast it was moving and whether it was traveling in a herd.

▽ **Procompsognathus**

Plateosaurus — "flat lizard"

Plateosaurus [play-tee-uh-SAWR-us] was a twenty-foot-long (6 m) planteater that usually walked on two legs nibbling the leaves from the trees, but often walked on all fours to feed on ground plants. It had wide, five-toed feet and a sharp curved claw on the "thumb" of each hand. This thumb could be used to scrape leaves from the ground or from tree branches. It could also be used as a weapon to stab an attacker.

Its jaws were filled with triangular-shaped teeth. These teeth could shred plants, but could not grind them up the way molars do. It is possible that Plateosaurus swallowed stones that would then grind up the plants in its stomach. One paleontologist has suggested that when the stones were worn smooth, the dinosaur belched them up.

Coelophysis — "hollow form"

Coelophysis [see-lo-FISE-iss] was definitely built for speed. This active two-legged hunter had hollow bones, just like a bird, which made it light. It had a long, flexible neck, a narrow skull and a very long tail. Running swiftly on birdlike feet and legs through the forest underbrush, it pursued lizards, dragonflies, small mammals and frogs, catching them in its grasping, three-fingered hands. The dinosaur's mouth was lined with many sharp, sawblade teeth. Large eye openings in the skull show that Coelophysis had keen eyesight.

Although Coelophysis was probably an ancestor of the giant meat-eater Tyrannosaurus, it was only the size of a large dog. It may have hunted in packs in order to prey on larger dinosaurs. Coelophysis was such an active animal that some scientists think it was warm-blooded.

Paleontologists were very excited when many Coelophysis skeletons were unearthed in a place known as Ghost Ranch, New Mexico. The group of adult and young dinosaurs had died together, perhaps trapped in quicksand or maybe smothered in a sandstorm. Finding them all together suggests that Coelophysis lived in family groups and took care of its young. Examining the bones of young and old dinosaurs from one family group gave scientists a picture of how a dinosaur grows.

Two of the dinosaur skeletons found had the bones of baby Coelophysis inside their rib cages. At first, the dinosaur detectives thought that these small skeletons must be embryos. But

▽ **Coelophysis**

the skeletons were too well-developed to be unborn babies. A better, but more disturbing, explanation is that the adults had eaten the babies. They probably ate any small creature they could catch!

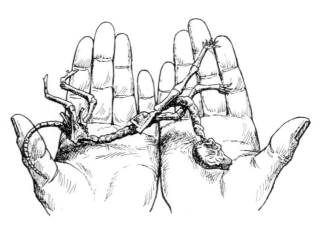

▽ **Mussaurus**

Mussaurus — "mouse lizard"

Mussaurus [moose-SAWR-us] was a tiny dinosaur, just eight inches long

35

(20.3 cm), small enough to hold in your hand. That's because it was just a baby! This hatchling, uncovered by fossil hunter José Bonaparte in Argentina, was probably a prosauropod, a predecessor to the giant sauropods of the Jurassic Period. The full skeleton was found in a nest with the remains of four other baby dinosaurs and some bits of eggshell. It is thought that baby Mussaurus and its brothers and sisters were still in the nest together because their parents were caring for them.

We don't know what an adult Mussaurus might look like because no remains have yet been found. Perhaps the parents of the mouse dinosaur were as big as elephants!

Heterodontosaurus — "different-toothed lizard"

Heterodontosaurus [het-er-uh-DON-tuh-sawr-us] was a small, two-legged plant-eater with an unusual feature. It had three different kinds of teeth. It had sharp front teeth and a horn-covered beak for biting, closely-spaced molars or cheek teeth for grinding, and two pairs of sharp, curved tusks, perhaps used for defense or to distinguish males from females. Its jaw could move not just up and down, but also side to side with the upper and lower jaws sliding over each other. Here was a dinosaur that could chew!

Theropods large and small, as well as thecodonts, probably preyed on these small creatures. In order to survive, they needed to be very fast and alert to danger.

▽ **Heterodontosaurus and Lesothosaurus, two early ornithopods.**

Lesothosaurus — "Lesotho lizard"

Lesothosaurus [les-o-toe-SAWR-us], like Heterodontosaurus, was one of the earliest ornithopods ("bird feet"). It was a fast, two-legged plant-eater, a mere thirty-five inches long (89 cm), with light bones and leaf-shaped, serrated teeth.

A scientist, Tony Thulborn, suggested that little Lesothosaurus may have aestivated. That means that it slept during the hot, dry season when there wasn't enough food.

Here are the clues: the skeletons of two lesothosaurs were found together— each one had brand-new teeth. Their old worn teeth were found nearby. The possible answer to the mystery: like other dinosaurs (and reptiles), Lesothosaurus's teeth were constantly replacing themselves. Since it took weeks after the old one dropped out for the new one to grow in, it looked like the two lesothosaurs must have been sleeping there for a long time before being buried.

But then another scientist, Jim Hopson, took a good hard look at the evidence for that theory. Among the teeth that had fallen out was a tooth of another kind of dinosaur. Perhaps the bones and teeth had washed down from other places. In that case, they may not have belonged to the two lesothosaurs at all. It seems that the aestivating theory needs more evidence before it can be proved.

37

5
DINOSAURS OF THE JURASSIC PERIOD

△ **Ornitholestes**

Ornitholestes — "bird robber"

Ornitholestes [or-nith-o-LESS-teez] was about six feet long (1.8 m) and walked on two long, birdlike legs. This theropod was a swift runner with leg muscles and ankle joints built for speed and maneuverability. Each hand had three clawed fingers with one finger that moved like a thumb to allow the dinosaur to grasp.

Ornitholestes is often depicted chasing Archaeopteryx, the first bird, although there is no proof that the two ever lived in the same part of the world. The "bird robber" more likely ate lizards, frogs and small ratlike mammals that it caught in its deadly grip. Its jaws contained big, sharp, curved teeth and strong muscles that gave it a powerful bite.

An almost complete skeleton of Ornitholestes was found at Bone Cabin Quarry in Wyoming. Judging from the rather large ear, eye and nostril holes in the skull, scientists believe that Ornitholestes had very keen eyesight, hearing and sense of smell. These heightened senses and speed helped it hunt small game and escape danger. Perhaps the only robbing Ornitholestes did was from the kills of other larger predators.

Allosaurus — "different lizard"

Allosaurus [AL-uh-sawr-us] was a meat-eating dinosaur big and powerful enough to prey on the giant sauropods Apatosaurus and Brachiosaurus. It was thirty-five feet long (10.6 m) and tall enough to reach a second story window.

Allosaurus was bipedal (walked on two feet), like all theropods. Powerful leg muscles enabled it to run as fast as a man, even though it weighed in at three to four tons (2.7 to 3.6 t). We know from fossilized footprints that it had a six-foot (1.8 m) stride. Each foot had three sharp talons. Its arms were quite short, with three clawed fingers on each hand.

A short, sturdy neck supported Allosaurus's massive head. Its large eyes were shaded by bony crests on the brow. Strong jaw muscles and four-inch-long (10 cm) serrated teeth were the weapons it needed to pierce the tough leathery skins of the sauropods. Allosaurus, like many dinosaurs, had an endless supply of teeth. Even if a tooth broke off, another one quickly grew in its place. Its jaw was hinged to open very wide so that it could swallow large pieces of flesh or an entire animal.

Stegosaurus — "plated lizard"

Stegosaurus [STEG-uh-sawr-us] was a four-footed, plant-eating dinosaur that probably grazed in herds. It is best known for the row of spectacular leaf-shaped plates that ran down its neck, back and partway down its tail. The biggest plates were often two feet tall (60.9 cm).

What the plates were for remains a mystery. Were they protective armor against predators like Allosaurus? The evidence shows that the plates were not attached to the backbone, but were only embedded in the skin. This leads some scientists to believe that the plates may have stuck out sideways; others think they stood straight up. In either case they would not protect the flanks or belly of a slow-moving stegosaurus from sharp teeth and claws.

Maybe the plates were to make the eleven-foot-tall (3.3 m) dinosaur look bigger to its enemies. Maybe they were to help stegosaurs recognize each other when they were looking for mates. A close look at the plates reveals a clue. Each hollow plate has a web of tiny grooves that at one time contained blood vessels. This would make the plates ideal solar panels. They could collect heat and warm the dinosaur's blood. Then for cooling the body, the plates would act as radiators, giving off the heat.

Scientists wanted to test this idea, so they placed a model of a stegosaur in a wind tunnel and found that the row of alternating plates was the best design to use cooling breezes. It seems a good guess that Stegosaurus had its own built-in heating and cooling system.

At Dinosaur National Monument in Utah, the fossil skeletons of two baby stegosaurs were found. Paleontologists were excited because very few baby dinosaurs of any kind have been discovered. These babies did not have plates on their backs. Perhaps stegosaurs did not grow the plates until they were adults.

Stegosaurus had a remarkably small head for its body size. The sixteen-inch-long (40.6 cm) head had a horn-covered beak for cropping ground plants like ferns and horsetails that grew in open areas. Its jaw was weak and its teeth were not meant for grinding, so it is possible that it depended on belly stones to digest the plant matter. Stegosaurus had such a tiny mouth that it makes one wonder how it could have eaten enough to fuel its twenty-five-foot-long (7.6 m) body.

Apatosaurus — "deceptive lizard"

Apatosaurus [ah-PAT-uh-sawr-us] is the name that fossil hunter Marsh gave

▷ Footprints show that young apatosaurs walked in the inside of the group, surrounded by adults who protected them from predators.

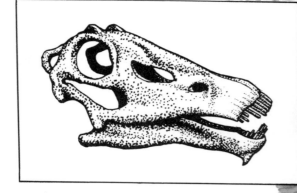

△ Skull of an apatosaur

to a huge plant-eating dinosaur he discovered. Then he found the bones of what he thought was another dinosaur and called it Brontosaurus. He didn't know that both skeletons were from the same kind of dinosaur. Scientists now use the first name, Apatosaurus.

Several almost complete skeletons of apatosaurs have been unearthed, but for many years no skull was found. Paleontologists guessed that the head was short and boxy like the head of another sauropod, Camarasaurus. But in 1979, when an authentic Apatosaurus skull was studied, scientists found out that its head was long and slender. Apatosaurus reconstructions in some museums still have the wrong head!

The Apatosaurus weighed about thirty tons (27.2 t) and walked on four legs and feet. Fossilized footprints show that Apatosaurus's foot was three feet wide. Its front legs were shorter than the back ones so that the back arched, ending in a thirty-foot (9 m), whiplike tail. Its long, thick neck towered twenty feet (6 m) in the air. Blunt, peglike teeth just in the front of the mouth nipped the topmost twigs and needles from pine and fir trees.

Because it had no molars, Apatosaurus swallowed its food whole. It also swallowed stones that ground up the plant matter in its stomach until the stones were worn smooth. The dinosaur's nostrils were set high on the head so that the airway would bypass the mouth. This way it could browse and breathe at the same time.

Apatosaurus's brain was human size. It had keen eyesight and a keen sense of smell, which were important in detecting the presence of its worst enemy, the ferocious meat-eater, Allosaurus.

There is evidence, too, that apatosaurs traveled in herds for protection. Fossil footprints of apatosaurs show that the younger dinosaurs walked in the middle of a group shielded by the larger adults. How can a herd of apatosaurs walk together without stepping on each other's tails? The answer is that their tails did not touch the ground. Strong muscles in the tail held it straight out and also enabled it to lash at attackers.

Camptosaurus — "bent lizard"

The most common plant-eater on the Jurassic plains was flat-headed Camptosaurus [KAMP-tuh-sawr-us]. Camptosaurus got its name because it walked on its hind legs, but often bent down on all fours to feed. Solidly built arms, wide hands, strong wrist bones and possibly hooved fingers enabled it to support its weight while cropping

the ferns with its horned-covered beak.

It may have had a long, curling tongue like a giraffe's that could pull the leaves from taller plants into its mouth and across the bony ridge in the front of its bottom jaw. Efficient grinding teeth were tightly packed in the

42

nosaur. Barely two feet long (60.9 cm) and weighing six or seven pounds (2.7 or 3.2 kg), it was no bigger than a modern-day chicken. In fact, its long, scaly legs and three-toed, clawed feet resembled a bird's. It had a small head, long neck and, like a tyrannosaur, two clawed fingers on each hand. A long tail served as its balancing rod when it was running full tilt. Its small jaw was lined with many pointed teeth.

An especially good fossil skeleton of Compsognathus shows small bones in the stomach of the dinosaur that proved to be lizard bones.

Besides fleet-footed lizards, it hunted small mammals and insects, catching and holding them in its grasping hands. Large eyesockets in its skull show that Compsognathus had good eyesight.

There are a lot of similarities in the skeletons of Compsognathus and Archaeopteryx, the first bird. Some scientists believe that, like Archaeopteryx, Compsognathus may have been a dinosaur with feathers!

Brachiosaurus — "arm lizard"

For many years, Brachiosaurus [BRAK-ee-uh-sawr-us] held the record for the largest and heaviest known land animal. It weighed over eighty tons (725 t)—as much as twelve full-grown elephants! It was seventy-five feet long (22.8 m) from its short snout to the tip of its tail.

Unlike other giant sauropods of the Jurassic Period, Brachiosaurus was built a bit like a giraffe, with its front legs longer than its back legs so that its back sloped towards the ground. It had a big, barrel-shaped body to hold its

back of the jaw. A bony palate that separated the airways of the mouth and nose let Camptosaurus chew and breathe at the same time. Large cheeks served as a food storage area so that the dinosaur could chew food over and over again before swallowing.

Camptosaurus had a spurlike claw on each hand and could run swiftly when there was danger. But a camptosaur's best defense against packs of meat-eating hunters was to travel in herds.

Compsognathus — "pretty jaw"

Compsognathus [COMP-so-NAY-thus] was the smallest meat-eating di-

enormous stomach, a very long neck and a relatively short tail.

An unusual feature on Brachiosaurus's head poses another mystery for dinosaur detectives. There were two very large nostrils in the bony crest on top of its head! Suppose these nostrils acted like a snorkel. Suppose this extremely heavy animal spent a lot of time in the water. The water would make its body lighter and was a safe place from predators. Wouldn't this snorkel on its head be the ideal way to breathe while standing on the bottom of a lake?

Many scientists accepted this picture of Brachiosaurus's lifestyle until someone pointed out a mistake. It would be impossible to stand in deep water and breathe through a snorkel. The water pressure would have collapsed Brachiosaurus's lungs and the blood vessels in its neck. In fact, it is now believed that brachiosaurs spent most of their time on dry land feeding on the needles from the tops of the trees.

Why did Brachiosaurus have nostrils on the top of its head? Membranes inside the nasal cavity might have vibrated so that brachiosaurs could call to each other when there was danger. Imagine what that call sounded like . . .

In 1972, a new record breaker for largest and heaviest land animal was discovered. Fossil hunter Jim Jensen uncovered an eight-foot-long (2.4 m) shoulderblade and a five-foot-long (1.5 m) neck bone at Dry Mesa Quarry in Colorado. If, as he thought, he discovered a species of Brachiosaurus, then this dinosaur he named Supersaurus must have been fifty feet tall (15 m), the biggest dinosaur yet.

But wait! Then Dinosaur Jim, as he is called, found a nine-foot-long (2.7 m) shoulder bone. This dinosaur, Ultrasaurus, stood sixty feet high (18 m), taller than a six-story building!

Both dinosaurs were giant planteating sauropods who once roamed the forests of Jurassic North America.

▷ **Ultrasaurus**

44

6

DINOSAURS OF THE EARLY CRETACEOUS PERIOD

Deinonychus — "terrible claws"

Though Deinonychus [dyne-ON-ik-us] was the most ferocious predatory dinosaur of all time, it wasn't massive or muscle-bound. Instead it was very fast and cunning and had a new method of killing—with its feet!

Deinonychus stood about five feet tall (1.5 m), the size of an average sixth grader. It was twelve feet long (3.6 m) and ran on two toes of its strong bird-like legs. But it was the murderous weapon on its middle toe that was the key to Deinonychus's success as a killer: a five-inch-long (12.7 cm), razor sharp, sickle-shaped claw used to slash open the bellies of its prey. The toe could bend backwards to lift the claw off the ground and protect its point when Deinonychus was running.

Besides long arms and long-fingered, grasping hands, Deinonychus had an unusual wrist structure that let the hands rotate, so that the palms could face each other for grabbing and holding struggling prey.

Its tail was stiffened by long, bony rods and stuck out straight behind its body. The tail could move not only side to side, like other dinosaurs' tails, but also up and down. In this way it acted as a stabilizer and allowed Deinonychus to make quick changes in

△ The "terrible claw"

direction when chasing and attacking its prey.

All these features added up to an efficient killing machine. Scientists believe this was the mode of attack: Deinonychus would sneak up on a victim, leap upon it and hold it at arms' length in its strong grip. Then, while balanced on one leg, it would deliver powerful kicks with the other foot, slashing the animal's underbelly with its foot claw.

Nothing was more dangerous than a deinonychus, except a hunting pack of deinonychus! Fossil evidence shows that these intelligent animals cooperated in bringing down large game. Five deinonychus skeletons were found with the remains of a tenontosaur, a plant-

45

eater that when full-grown weighed al-most two tons (1.8 t). They probably waited for the young or sick dinosaurs to stray from the herd.

Although Deinonychus was one of the fastest animals on earth during the Early Cretaceous, it had to depend on surprise and cunning to catch a fleet-footed ornithopod. It may have had blotchy or spotted skin that camou-flaged it.

▽**A hunting pack of deinonychus bring down a young tenontosaurus.**

Deinonychus did not use its teeth for killing like other meat-eating dino-saurs, but instead used them mostly for eating. Its teeth were serrated and curved inward. Strong muscles clamped the jaw shut so the neck could pull back, tearing chunks of flesh from a carcass. As in other carnivorous dino-saurs, there may have been a built-in shock absorber behind the eyes to pro-tect the brain from being jarred when the jaws snapped shut.

The discovery of this very active running and leaping dinosaur made scientists wonder whether it was warm-blooded. One paleontologist sug-

gested that warm-blooded Deinonychus may have had feathers to hold in its body heat.

Tenontosaurus — "tendon lizard"

This fast and agile ornithopod was longer than your living room and weighed as much as two tons (1.8 t). It walked on all fours to feed, but could run swiftly on its long hind legs. A long tail stiffened with bony rods counterbalanced its heavy chest when fleeing from its worst enemy, Deinonychus. As it ran, the stabilizing tail let Tenontosaurus swerve from side to side to avoid its predators' lunges. The tail may also have served as a defense, lashing out when cornered by a pack of attackers.

Although Tenontosaurus was fast for a dinosaur of its size, it had few defenses against its many predators. Traveling in herds provided some safety, but perhaps protective coloring, such as a dappled skin color to blend in with the landscape, helped Tenontosaurus to slip past danger.

Sauropelta — "lizard shield"

Sauropelta [sar-o-PELT-a] belongs to a family of plant-eating dinosaurs called nodosaurs ("node lizards"). Nodosaurs were part of a larger group of dinosaurs classified as ankylosauria, or armored dinosaurs, sometimes called the tanks of the dinosaur world. Bony plates covered their backs, sides, tails and even their heads. Scientists know from fossilized skin that these bony "nodes" formed the texture of the skin.

Sauropelta was one of the largest nodosaurs. It was twenty-five feet long (7.6 m) and weighed about three and a half tons (3.1 t). It walked on four short legs, the hind legs a bit longer than the front ones, so that the back was curved. Long, sharp spikes poked out from its sides. Its armored head was long and narrow with a horn-covered beak and a small mouth. Sauropelta may have been a picky eater, feeding only on certain ground plants.

While other dinosaurs depended on long legs and speed or camouflage to escape danger, Sauropelta's greatest protection from meat-eaters was its suit of armor. When an enemy approached, Sauropelta simply fell to the ground to cover its legs and soft belly.

No predator, not even Deinonychus with its terrible claws, could pierce its bony armor. The only way to kill a nodosaur was to turn it over on its back. Even a pack of strong carnosaurs could not lift 7,000 pounds (3,175 kg)!

Iguanodon — "iguana tooth"

The first dinosaur bones to be studied by scientists belonged to Iguanodon [ig-WAN-o-don]. In 1822, Mary Ann Mantell picked up some unusual fossil teeth from a rock pile by the side of a road in Sussex, England. Mrs. Mantell was familiar with fossils. She had made hundreds of detailed drawings of them for her husband's book, *The Fossils of the South Downs*. She showed the teeth to Dr. Mantell, who was an avid fossil collector, and as it turned out, one of the first dinosaur detectives. He traced the rock pile where the teeth had been found to a nearby quarry and enlisted the help of the quarrymen to find any other remains. More bones and a horn were uncovered.

Dr. Mantell was puzzled by the triangular-shaped, serrated teeth. He searched museums for teeth of any animal, living or extinct, that might resemble them. At last he found the teeth of an iguana, a lizard from Central America. They had the same shape but were much smaller. Mantell decided that the teeth and bones must belong to a huge plant-eating reptile which he named Iguanodon.

Mantell had very few clues to go on. When Iguanodon was reconstructed, it had four stout elephantlike legs and a horn on the end of its snout like a rhinoceros.

In 1878, coal miners in Bernissart, Belgium made a startling discovery. In a layer of clay above a coal seam, 1,056 feet (321.8 m) underground, they found the skeletons of thirty-nine adult iguanodons, many of them complete. Here was a rare opportunity to compare the anatomy of individual dinosaurs, male and female, of the same species.

Belgian paleontologist Louis Dollo spent the next twenty-five years carefully studying the bones of the iguanodons and the fossils of the insects, plants and animals found in the rock strata with them. His step-by-step ap-

Mary Ann Mantell

Dr. Gideon Mantell

▷ Early dinosaur detectives, with few clues to go on, guessed that Iguanodon's spike grew out of its snout like the horn of a rhinocerous.

▷ Today we know that the spike belonged on Iguanodon's thumb.

proach to the study of the iguanodons, their posture, feeding habits and environment, set the standard for all dinosaur investigations that followed.

Dollo discovered that Iguanodon was twenty-five feet long (7.6 m) and stood twelve to fifteen feet tall (3.6 to 4.5 m). It walked on two three-toed legs, sometimes going down on all fours to feed. Iguanodon's five-fingered hand could flex, but not grip. Some of the fingers may have had horny hooves rather than claws. At right angles to the fingers was a sharp, spiky thumb. (It was this thumb spike that earlier dinosaur detectives had put on Iguanodon's snout!) The thumb could have been used as a stabbing weapon at close quarters or in mating.

The fact that none of the thirty-nine iguanodons was a juvenile suggests that these dinosaurs may have raised and protected their young in a special nesting ground until they were large enough to accompany the herd.

Iguanodon was a plant-eater. In fact, it may have been the first dinosaur to eat the flowering plants that were beginning to appear in the Early Cretaceous Period. The secret to this was efficient chewing. Iguanodon was equipped with a sharp beak for nipping and many closely-packed grinding cheek teeth. The upper and lower jaws slid past each other, chopping and crushing the tough plants.

Like its predecessor Camptosaurus, Iguanodon's skull was long and flat. A cast of the inside of the skull, called an "endocranial cast," shows the shape of a large brain and channels for blood vessels and nerves.

The remains of Iguanodon-type dinosaurs have been found on almost every continent. Herds of grazing iguanodons must have been a common sight in the Early Cretaceous world.

7

DINOSAURS OF THE LATE CRETACEOUS PERIOD

▷ The biggest meat-eating dinosaur, Tyrannosaurus rex.

Tyrannosaurus — "tyrant lizard"

Everyone, it seems, has heard of Tyrannosaurus [tie-RAN-uh-sawr-us], the biggest meat-eating dinosaur. But the world's most popular dinosaur could also be called the dinosaur with the split personality! Was it a ferocious and cunning hunter feared by every creature that shared its world? Or was it a slow and clumsy animal who survived by eating carcasses?

Scientists can't agree on how Tyrannosaurus behaved. Fortunately, the remains of this dinosaur have been particularly well-preserved, so scientists know more about what it looked like than any other theropod.

Tyrannosaurus was forty feet long (12 m) and stood over eighteen feet tall (5.4 m). Its skull was four feet long, thick and heavy. Muscles attached to spines on the neckbones and ribcage let Tyrannosaurus turn and lift its massive head. Huge jaws were lined with six-inch-long (15.2 cm), curved teeth. Its arms were extremely short. In fact, Tyrannosaurus couldn't touch its chin!

Each hand had only two clawed fingers.

The pelvic bones were large, with plenty of room for the big muscles and heavy-boned legs necessary to carry a tyrannosaur's six-ton (5.4 t) weight. It walked or ran on two wide, three-taloned feet, bent over with its tail straight out behind to balance the weight.

Because of its great size and weight, a tyrannosaur's hunting style was simple. Like a land shark, it opened its massive jaws and ran at the victim. Its head was designed to take the impact of the charge. Because its short arms were useless to hold struggling prey, the tyrannosaur had to depend on the strength of its jaws and teeth. Like many other dinosaurs (and sharks), Tyrannosaurs had an endless supply of replacement teeth that would erupt from its gums whenever a tooth was broken off.

Other theropods had short arms, but scientists wondered why a tyrannosaur's arms were so ridiculously short. Of what use could they be? This is what one dinosaur detective concluded. Suppose a two-legged creature like Tyrannosaurus lay down to take a nap after a heavy meal. How would it ever get up again? If it pushed with its feet, the front part of the body would slide and its face would plow up the dirt. But if it could keep the front of its body from sliding with clawed hands, the mighty legs could come up under the rest of the body. By straightening its knees, Tyrannosaurus could be upright again.

A few paleontologists who have studied the hip joints and leg bones of Tyrannosaurus say that the huge carnosaur could not have run. In fact, they insist that Tyrannosaurus's stride wasn't much larger than the size of its foot—it shuffled more than walked.

Perhaps tyrannosaurs wandered in pairs, sniffing for the blood of animals that had already died from natural causes, from accidents or from attack by other predators. Even though smaller meat-eaters might have worked hard to catch a dinner, just the appearance of two enormous tyrannosaurs, their mouths full of sharp teeth, would probably have scared them away from their kills. Then the "tyrant lizards" could eat in peace.

Pachycephalosaurus — "thick-headed lizard"

Pachycephalosaurus [pak-ee-SEF-uh-lo-sawr-us] belongs to a group of dinosaurs called "boneheads." These dinosaurs had built-in crash helmets! The bone on top of Pachycephalosaurus's two-foot-long skull formed a dome nearly ten inches (25 cm) thick. It was fringed with bony knobs and short spikes. Boneheads needed thick skulls to protect their brains from sudden impact.

Think of mountain goats and bighorn sheep and you will have a good idea of how the pachycephalosaurs lived. It is thought that herds roamed the hills and mountains, browsing in an area where carnosaurs, such as Tyrannosaurus, rarely came. Perhaps each group was led and protected by a strong male. All of the females of the group belonged to him. If another male wanted to take over, the leader and the challenger would have a head-butting battle to see who would rule the group. With their backs and tails flat, heads down, the two males would charge at each other, their thick skulls smashing together until one male proved· to be stronger.

Dinosaur detectives examined the way the bone cells grew in the boneheads' skulls. They found that cells radiated out from the center of the dome. The center, then, was the area of the skull meant to take the most stress. With a straight back, the shock of head-crashing traveled through the dome and was absorbed by the backbone. The brain was not damaged by the blows.

Inside the dome, the brain was rather small, smaller than a mountain goat's. But Pachycephalosaurus had keen eyesight and an excellent sense of smell. It had short, sharp teeth for eating leaves, seeds, fruits and maybe insects which it uncovered by digging with the bony knobs on its small snout.

Hadrosaurs — "big lizards"

The most numerous dinosaurs in the Late Cretaceous Period were the hadrosaurs, or "duckbill" dinosaurs.

These gentle plant-eaters probably had no way to defend themselves against predators. They weren't extremely large or fast runners. They had no sharp horns, armor, lashing tail or even a thumb spike like their ancestor Iguanodon. How did they survive and become so plentiful?

Part of the answer may have been their teeth! As the world became covered with many kinds of flowering plants, hadrosaurs developed the teeth to grind up the hard-to-chew leaves, twigs, seeds and fruits.

Duckbill teeth were arranged in many tightly-packed rows, forming a grinding surface like that of a metal file. Underneath the more than 100 working teeth were new teeth ready to push out and replace the worn ones. A duckbill may have had up to 2,000 teeth in its jaws, both working and re-

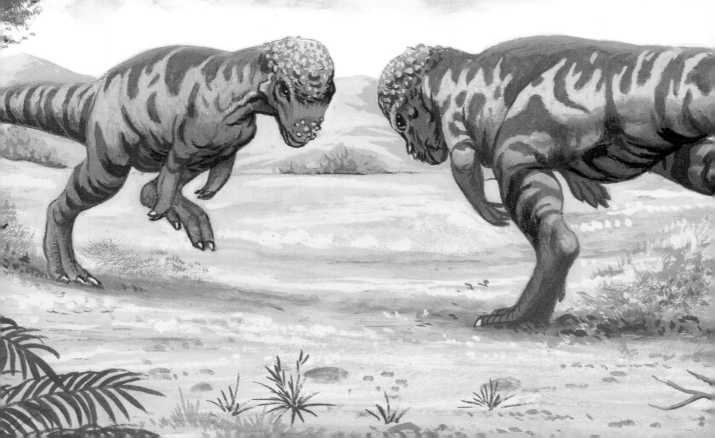

placement teeth, at any one time. Imagine how many teeth a duckbill used in its lifetime! These grinding surfaces, combined with strong jaw muscles, let duckbills eat tough foods that other dinosaurs could not digest. The forests could support greater numbers of hadrosaurs.

Although there were several different kinds of duckbill dinosaurs, the body designs were very similar. They were medium large plant-eaters who could stand on two legs to reach tree branches or go on all fours to graze on ground plants. Their legs and arms were long and thin. The feet were wide and had three hooved toes. The tail was long and tall. The fingers on each hand may have been webbed.

The difference among hadrosaurs was in the shape of the "duckbill" and the fantastic bony crests on the top of their heads. At one time, dinosaur detectives who tried to answer the riddle of the duckbill's beak and crest came up with an answer that seemed to fit. Suppose a duckbill, they said, was like the ducks of today and spent a lot of time in the water. When chased by its enemies, the defenseless duckbill could escape into deep water. Its webbed fingers could push through the water like paddles. Its tall tail could help it swim. The teeth in its mouth were always falling

◁ **Rival pachycephalosaurs butt heads.**

▽ **Skull of a pachycephalosaur**

53

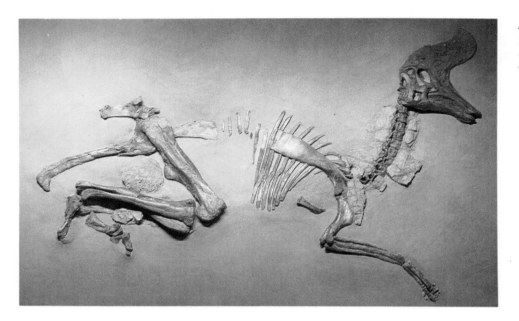

out, so they must have been weak and only strong enough to crush up mushy water plants. The curious nasal crest was really an airway that worked like a snorkel or an airtank to let the dinosaur breathe underwater.

The trouble with the idea of hadrosaurs as water dwellers is that none of the evidence will "hold water!" First, the webbed fingers would make a paddle too small to propel a large dinosaur through the water. A tail built for swimming would have to be able to wiggle. A duckbill's tail was encased in bony tendons that wouldn't wiggle. The tendons formed a structure like a cantilever bridge to hold up the tail and balance the upper part of the body when the dinosaur was walking or running on two legs.

Next, the teeth were not weak, but superior teeth for grinding tough material. The "duckbill" was more like a sharp slicing surface. In fact, when paleontologists discovered a mummified hadrosaur, the contents of its stomach showed that it ate pine needles and twigs, not mushy water plants.

Finally, the hollow crest could not have been a snorkel because there was no hole in it. As an airtank it would have held a very small amount of air—not enough to inflate the dinosaur's lungs.

But why did many hadrosaurs have big, curiously-shaped bony crests on their heads?

Corythosaurus [ko-RITH-uh-sawrus], the "helmet lizard," had a tall, thin crest that looked like a big disk set on end. Air passages ran from the nostrils, looped up through the crest and ended in the back of the throat. The male corythosaurs had bigger crests than the females.

Lambeosaurus [LAM-bee-uh-sawrus], or "Lambe's lizard," had a crest that has been described as hatchetlike.

A thin, squarish piece of bone aimed forward between the eyes while a long piece, the handle of the hatchet, aimed towards the back of the head.

Tsintaosaurus [Tzin-TAY-o-sawr-us], or "Tsintao lizard," had a long, bony spike protruding forward from between its eyes like the horn of a unicorn. A piece of skin may have stretched between the horn and the dinosaur's snout.

The most amazing crest of all belonged to Parasaurolophus [par-uh-sawr-OL-uh-fus], the "similar-crested lizard." The crest was a long, gracefully sweeping horn that started at the nose and extended back as much as six feet (1.8 m)!

We already know that the crests were not snorkels or airtanks, yet they were hooked up to the breathing system. The best idea so far is that the crests were resonators. Sounds made by the dinosaur vibrated inside the bony crest like air going through a bugle. A mating call or distress signal may have been loud!

But what does a hadrosaur sound like? David Weishampel, a professor at The Johns Hopkins University School of Medicine, once built a life-size model of a parasaurolophus crest out of plastic tubing. When he blew through it, out came a low, loud honk, a sound somewhere between a goose and a fog horn.

Spinosaurus — "spine lizard"

Spinosaurus [SPY-nuh-sawr-us] was a great two-legged carnosaur that was forty feet long (12 m) and weighed more than seven tons (6.3 t). Its head was large and full of long, sharp, straight teeth. But it was what Spinosaurus wore on its back that gave it its name. Sticking straight up from each vertebra along its backbone were huge spines, some as high as a tall man. These spines were covered in a sheet of skin to form a big fin in the shape of a sail.

Paleontologists have several ideas about how Spinosaurus used this enormous sail. One idea is that it was a way

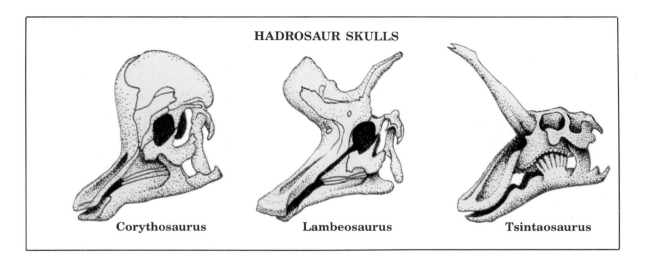

HADROSAUR SKULLS

Corythosaurus   Lambeosaurus   Tsintaosaurus

for rival males to show off in order to get mates. Males had to be careful only to show off and not to fight, because the skin sail was not sturdy enough to hold together in a prolonged attack.

Another idea is that the blood that went through the skin of the sail was warmed by the sun. By catching the sun's morning rays, a cold-blooded spinosaur could warm up and become active early in the day while other cold-blooded prey were still sluggish.

Even if Spinosaurus was not an active hunter but a scavenger searching the hot plains for carcasses, the sail could help cool its blood. By facing into the sun or catching a breeze in its sail, the sail could radiate the extra body heat more quickly. This temperature regulation system of solar collector and radiator is like the one used by Stegosaurus and its bony plates.

What we know or can guess about Spinosaurus comes from a few fossil bones found in Egypt. Unfortunately, the fossils were destroyed during World War II, so detectives can only get clues from illustrations and written descriptions of the bones.

△ **Spinosaurus may have used its sail as a solar collector and radiator.**

Ceratopsians — "horned face"

Ceratopsians were the last dinosaurs to develop and the very last ones to die out. They were also the most common dinosaurs during the Late Cretaceous Period in North America.

The best way to describe the ceratopsian body design is "rhinoceros-like." Ceratopsians evolved from two-legged dinosaurs. They became four-footed perhaps because their heads became too heavy, or because cropping low-growing plants on all fours allowed a heavy head to develop.

The ceratopsians' heads were huge. In some species, they were one-third the length of the body. Long, sharp brow and nasal horns and great, bony neck frills made them look even larger. Attached to the neck frill were powerful jaw muscles that moved the dinosaur's parrot beak. Inside the cheeks were rows and rows of teeth, similar to the teeth arrangement of hadrosaurs. Ceratopsian teeth, however, did not grind. They worked like scissors to slice hard-to-chew food such as palm fronds.

While the ceratopsian had armor and weapons on its neck and head, the back and flanks were unprotected, so a ceratopsian had to face its enemy to defend itself. It may have charged like a rhinoceros, head down, ready to stab with its horn(s). Perhaps just shaking its huge head was enough to discourage most predators. Even a tyrannosaur would have hesitated when it saw those dangerous horns. If the carnosaur failed to kill with the first bite, the ceratopsian would be close enough to gore it.

The lifestyle of this aggressive plant-eater was not solitary like the rhinoceros's. Ceratopsians lived more like buffalo or bison do, roaming the low hills in large herds. There were probably herd leaders who watched for danger and faced enemies. When threatened, the herd may have surrounded the young, the adults facing out to form a circle bristling with horns, the great male bulls up front. Predators who killed ceratopsians most likely ambushed the young when the herd was spread out feeding.

Protoceratops [pro-toe-SAIR-uh-tops], or "first horned face," is the earliest known horned dinosaur. Its horns were actually large bumps above the eyes and snout. It was six to seven feet long (1.8 to 2.1 m) and weighed 3,000 pounds (1,361 kg).

Protoceratops skeletons were discovered in the Gobi Desert in

△ **Protoceratops mother and nest.**

▽ **Skeleton of a triceratops**

▽**A herd of centrosaurs crosses a river.**

Mongolia. The find caused excitement worldwide because dinosaur detectives uncovered many nests full of the first known dinosaur eggs. Scientists had guessed that dinosaurs laid eggs, but they had never had direct evidence. The protoceratops eggs were laid in a circle with their rounded sides pointing outward, just as the female protoceratops had deposited them eighty million years ago!

A more recent find in Alberta, Canada revealed the remains of hundreds of centrosaurs [SEN-truh-sawrs], or "sharp point lizards." This twenty-foot-long (6 m) ceratopsian had a single nose horn that curved forward. Spines or knobs jutted out from the edges of the neck frill and, from the top of the frill, two tongue-shaped horns curved forward.

Although it is called a short-frilled ceratopsian, a centrosaur's head was five to six feet long (1.5 to 1.8 m) from beak to frill! The nose horn was eighteen inches long (45.7 cm) and sharp. Centrosaurus was larger than its predecessor, Protoceratops. It was taller than a man at the shoulders and weighed about three tons (2.7 t).

Triceratops [try-SAIR-uh-tops], or "three horned face," was the biggest horned dinosaur. It was twenty-five feet long (7.6 m), stood nearly ten feet tall (3 m) and weighed about six tons (5.4 t). A short nose horn stood out over its beak. Two very long horns protruded from above each eye.

Scars on some triceratops skeletons show that these animals sometimes locked horns with each other in combat the same way male deer do when they lock antlers and push to test who is the

discovered in a nest of fossilized protoceratops eggs in Mongolia. It appears that Oviraptor slipped into the nest to steal the eggs when the parents weren't looking, but an angry mother protoceratops discovered the thief and crushed its skull with one stamp of her foot.

Some dinosaur detectives think that Oviraptor has been falsely accused of egg stealing. They argue that this little dinosaur didn't eat eggs and probably never raided another dinosaur's nest.

▷ **Oviraptor, "the egg thief," escapes with a protoceratops egg.**

strongest.

Large herds of triceratops browsed the open plains of what is now Montana, Wyoming and Alberta, Canada right up until the end of the Mesozoic, when all the dinosaurs, and many other animals and plants, mysteriously died.

Oviraptor — "egg thief"

The remains of Oviraptor [o-vee-RAP-tor], its skull crushed, were first

Oviraptor's diet may not have included eggs, but its short beak and strong jaws were designed to break through very hard shells. Perhaps Oviraptor used its powerful bite to open mollusks and other shellfish. Scientists think it was an omnivorous creature; it ate meat, such as birds, lizards and insects, as well as plants. Its long arms and grasping hands could catch prey or pull down overhanging branches to reach berries and buds.

Oviraptor closely resembled birds

▷ Dromiceiomimus bore a striking resemblance to the modern-day ostrich. Both creatures are known for their speed.

in important ways. Its bones were hollow. It had a toothless beak. It ran on two long, slender legs with three-toed, chickenlike feet. Oviraptor even had a collarbone that looked like the wishbone of a bird. But instead of wings, Oviraptor had long, thin arms and very large hands. Each hand had three long, straight fingers with sharp, curved claws, just the right shape for digging around for eggs in a sandy protoceratops nest!

Dromiceiomimus — "emu mimic"

Dromiceiomimus [dro-miss-ee-o-MY-mus] was probably the fastest dinosaur of all time. By looking at the structure of its leg and ankle bones, scientists estimate that it could run at top speeds of over fifty miles (80 km) per hour. That's faster than a racehorse!

Called one of the "ostrich dinosaurs" because it so closely resembled this modern-day bird, Dromiceiomimus

had a small head with a broad, toothless beak, a long, slim neck and long, thin legs. It was ten feet (3 m) from the tip of its beak to the end of its tail, which struck straight out, level with its back.

To find food, Dromiceiomimus probably used its three-toed feet to scrape leaf litter from the forest floor and reveal lizards and insects. Then it grabbed them with its three long, clawed fingers.

Dromiceiomimus had larger eyes than any land animal alive today. Its extremely keen eyesight allowed the dinosaur to see and hunt the small mammals that emerged from their burrows at dusk. Sharp eyes also helped the ostrich dinosaur detect danger. No predator could outrun a dromiceiomimus unless it caught this dinosaur by surprise. Although Dromiceiomimus could run swiftly in one direction, it couldn't maneuver or dodge very well.

8

FLYING AND SWIMMING REPTILES

While dinosaurs were the undisputed reptile rulers of the land during the Mesozoic Era, other reptiles ruled the sea and sky. These reptiles were not dinosaurs, although some, like the pterosaurs, were related to dinosaurs.

Pterosaurs in the air

During the Triassic Period, while the dinosaurs were learning to run, an archosaur cousin was learning to fly. Pterosaurs [TAIR-uh-sawrs], or "wing lizards," were the first fliers other than insects. These amazingly light-framed creatures flapped through the skies over ocean and plains right up until the Late Cretaceous Period.

Considering the thinness of their bones and their airborne lifestyle, it is surprising that so many pterosaurs were fossilized. Most of these are preserved in layers of rock laid down by former oceans. This is because many pterosaurs probably fished the oceans like seabirds today, swooping down to scoop or spear their dinners from the surface of the water. Fossils of species that lived on land are not so plentiful. We do know that pterosaurs had a great range in size; the smallest was about the size of a sparrow, while the largest known species had a wingspan wider than a small aircraft!

▽ **Rhamphorhynchus, a long-tailed pterosaur.**

Endocranial casts of pterosaur skulls show that they had large brains, at least as large and complex as those of birds of today. Pterosaurs resembled birds in other ways, too. Like birds, they had hollow bones about as thick as a baseball card. To make them even lighter, they contained no marrow but were honeycombed with canals that connected air sacs in the bones to the lungs.

A pterosaur's hind legs and feet looked very much like the birdlike legs of a small theropod. Its hands had three clawed fingers and one extremely long fourth finger that supported the narrow, leathery wing. Stiff, gristly tissue formed a framework in the wing. This tissue was connected to muscles that could control its tension.

It's difficult for us to imagine that this impressive flying machine belonged to a reptile. For many years experts believed that pterosaurs could not flap their wings. They were pictured as badly-designed, broad-winged gliders that depended on hot air currents to stay in the air. Many thought that pterosaur wings were attached to their hind legs so that they could not walk on land. Their wing was believed to be so fragile that a tree branch or rock could tear an irreparable hole in it.

Thanks to the recent work of paleontologist Kevin Padian, we now know that a pterosaur had the necessary bone structure to flap its wings. It could not only walk easily on land, it could run with its wings tucked up and its tail counter-balancing the weight of its head.

If pterosaurs were cold-blooded reptiles, how could they withstand the windchill high in the air and still keep flapping? Why didn't the cold make them sluggish and cause them to drop out of the sky? The answer is that

△Pteranodons may have lived much like ocean birds do, flying over the water and catching fish in their beaks.

tailed. Rhamphorhynchus [ram-fo-RINK-us], or "prow beak," was one of the first long-tailed pterosaurs to be discovered. It had a long, slender head with sharp teeth lining its jaws and protruding outwards. Its neck was long and could curve in an "s" shape, allowing it to lay back on the body like a pelican's. Aiming its snout at fish below, the rhamphorhyncus could snap its head forward like a spear, snagging its prey on its long teeth. The pterosaur's body and tail were only eighteen inches (45.7 cm) long, but its wingspan was over four feet (1.2 m). On the end of the long stiff tail was a flat membrane that may have worked like a rudder to steer in the wind.

Another long-tail was Dimorphodon [die-MOR-fo-don], or "two-form tooth." It had several spiky teeth in the front of its mouth and many small teeth in the back. Its snout was very deep and was used to catch insects or small animals. Experts are not sure why a dimorphodon's snout was so high, but it has been suggested that perhaps it was brightly colored and served as a display to attract mates.

The group of short-tailed pterosaurs are called pterodactyls [tair-uh-DAK-tils], or "wing finger." Pterodactyls lived fifty million years after Rhamphorhynchus. Their heads were longer and thinner than the long-tailed variety and the neck was much longer. Some had a large, bony crest protruding from the back of the head. Wind tunnel experiments show that these crests could work as rudders for steering. It is also possible that they were used to identify potential mates and rivals.

Early pterodactyls were quite small, but by the Late Cretaceous Period many had gained enormous wingspans and very little additional weight.

pterosaurs were probably warm-blooded reptiles.

Scientists had a hunch that pterosaurs may have had fur or feathers to keep them warm. Their hunch proved right. In the 1970s, a Russian scientist, A. G. Sharov, discovered the fossil of a pterosaur from the Jurassic period. He called it Sordes pilosus [SORD-ess-pil-O-sus], which means "hairy devil." The fossil showed clear impressions of wings and long, dense fur!

There are two main types of pterosaurs: long-tailed and short-

The biggest of all, indeed the largest creature ever to fly, was Quetzalcoatlus [ket-sol-ko-AT-lus], named after the Aztec feathered serpent god. Douglas Lawson discovered this giant of the sky in 1972 in Texas. It appears to have had a wingspan of forty feet (12 m), wider than an airplane! Its long beak may have been used to punch holes in the mud to get at mollusks. Or perhaps it was a scavenger, using its altitude and keen eyesight to spot carcasses on the flat plains below.

Pteranodon [tair-RAN-o-don], or "winged and toothless," had a six-foot-long (1.8 m), narrow, toothless skull with a long, bony crest that counterbalanced it. Its body was about the size of a turkey and weighed thirty-three pounds (15 kg), while its wingspan was twenty-seven feet (8.2 m). Pteranodon lived much like the albatross of today, flying over open ocean and catching and storing fish in its throat pouch. It is quite possible that Pteranodon was covered in fur to keep it warm.

Pteradaustro [tair-uh-DAW-stro], or "southern wing," was a pteradactyl found in Argentina. Its jaws were lined with fine comb teeth that acted like a strainer. Pteradaustro flew along the surface of the water, skimming off plankton with its beak. Plankton, minute marine organisms, would catch in the creature's teeth. Modern whales sift the water for plankton in the same way, using their baleen. Another animal that strains organisms from the water is the flamingo. It gets its pink color by way of the food chain—red plankton is eaten by shrimp which make up a big part of the flamingo's diet. One paleontologist has suggested that if red plankton were a large part of a pteradaustro's diet, there may have been a pink pteradactyl in the skies above Argentina!

Without evidence, no one can prove that these flying reptiles were somber brown or gray, as they have often been pictured. In fact, if pterosaurs displayed the protective coloring of their modern counterparts, shore birds and ocean birds, they would be white to blend in with the sky. Perhaps they were black and white, with the black on the top, to disguise themselves from other predators when on the ground, and white on the bottom to camouflage them from below when they were airborne. The next time you see a monster movie with a pterosaur depicted as an evil creature in the sky, imagine instead that it was

▽ **Two future paleontologists learn about plesiosaurs.**

△ **Elasmosaurus**

could lunge its small head at a passing fish with lightning speed, catching its prey on pointed teeth. Although it could strike with a rapid movement, Elasmosaurus was probably a slow swimmer. It paddled near the surface of the water with its neck extended below, searching for food.

When it was time for them to lay their eggs in the sand, plesiosaurs may more likely a white (or pink!) furry creature that ate fish!

Reptiles in the sea

One of the largest ocean-going reptiles was the short-necked plesiosaur [PLEE-zee-uh-sawr], called Kronosaurus [KRO-nuh-sawr-us], or "crown lizard," found in Australia. This killer whale of the Mesozoic oceans had an enormous skull twelve feet (3.6 m) long, the biggest head of any known reptile. The barrel-shaped body was forty feet (12 m) long. Kronosaurus propelled itself through the water with its flippers, beating them up and down like a penguin or sea turtle. It hunted other plesiosaurs, giant turtles and large ammonites (squidlike creatures).

Elasmosaurus [ee-LAZ-muh-sawr-us], "thin-plated lizard," was a long-necked plesiosaur. Indeed, its neck was over twenty feet (6 m) long! Coiling its neck up like a snake, the elasmosaur

have used their flippers to pull themselves along on land like walruses.

Ichthyosaurs [IK-thee-uh-sawrs], or "fish lizards," swam in the oceans as early as the Triassic Period. Their appearance and habits resemble those of the porpoises of today. An ichthyosaur had a very streamlined, smooth body and a long tail with a vertical tail fin. Its neckless head had large eyes and a long, thin snout lined with small, spiky teeth. The front limbs were flippers that did not propel the reptile as much as steer its course through the water.

Unlike plesiosaurs, ichthyosaurs could not venture on land, even to lay eggs. Instead, they bore live young who emerged from the mother ready to swim.

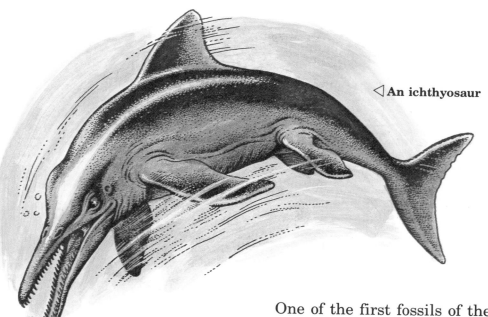

◁ An ichthyosaur

Temnodontosaurus [TEM-no-dont-uh-sawr-us], or "cutting-tooth lizard" was a thirty-foot (9 m) ichthyosaur from the early Jurassic that preyed on large fish and sometimes pterosaurs. One well-preserved skeleton shows unborn babies in a temnodontosaur's body cavity. One of the babies was just emerging, tail first, when the mother died and was fossilized.

▽A mosasaur devours an ammonite.

One of the first fossils of the Dinosaur Age to be discovered was of a marine reptile called a mosasaur [MO-zuh-sawr], or "Meuse lizard," after the Meuse River in Holland where it was found. Mosasaurs appeared in the Late Cretaceous Period and were formidable hunters. Scientists believe that these dragons of the sea were related to the modern monitor lizard.

Tylosaurus [TIE-lo-sawr-us], or "knot lizard," is the largest known mosasaur. Its thin body was twenty to thirty feet (6 to 9 m) long, including a tail that propelled it through the water. Webbed hands and feet were used for steering.

Its head was long, with four-foot-long (1.2 m) jaws and sharp teeth that could make short work of fish, ammonites and even giant sea turtles. Scientists know that it ate ammonities because they have found ammonite shells that bear the mosasaur's teethmarks.

Pterosaurs, plesiosaurs, ichthyosaurs and mosasaurs shared the Mesozoic world with the dinosaurs of the land. They also shared the dinosaur's fate. By the end of the Mesozoic Era, all these once-abundant reptiles disappeared from land, ocean and sky forever.

9

THE GREAT DYING

No one knows why all the dinosaurs disappeared from the face of the earth. Nevertheless, dinosaur detectives and other mystery lovers never seem to tire of thinking of ways to explain what could have happened sixty-five million years ago to push the successful dinosaurs to extinction. There is very little evidence to prove any of the theories. One fact we know from the fossil evidence is that dinosaurs were not the only creatures to disappear at the end of the Cretaceous. So many species of animals and plants died out during this time that scientists call it "The Great Dying."

Nearly three-quarters of all the species living on land and sea during the last million years of the Mesozoic Era were extinct when it ended. All large land animals were wiped out. Pterosaurs disappeared from the skies. Many, many plants died out, as did most species of marine plankton, the base of the food chain in the oceans. Ichthyosaurs, plesiosaurs and mosasaurs soon followed.

Some scientists suggest that a force drastically changed conditions on the earth. Animals and plants had no time to adapt. For many, the world became uninhabitable in a short time, and they died in great numbers.

Cosmic rays

One sudden-catastrophe theory says that a nearby star exploded. The super-

◁ Some scientists think that air pollution from volcanic eruptions held in the sun's heat and caused a worldwide climate change at the end of the Cretaceous Period.

nova sent shock waves strong enough to reverse the magnetic poles on the earth. This disruption allowed a great burst of deadly cosmic rays to enter the earth's atmosphere, killing many plants and animals. The theory asserts that bare-skinned dinosaurs were wiped out by radiation poisoning.

The iridium discovery

Geologist Walter Alvarez made an important discovery in Italy while studying the limestone layers there dating from the late Cretaceous Period. He found a layer of rock dating back to before the end of the Cretaceous that was full of fossils. This layer was topped by a thin layer of grayish-red clay in which there were very, very few fossils. This abrupt end to so much life was followed by another rock layer that was full of fossils of many new species.

Alvarez examined the empty clay layer sandwiched between the two life-filled ones. He found that the clay contained high amounts of an element called iridium. Iridium is a rare element on earth but is many times more plentiful in meteorites. By taking samples of this clay layer from different

▽ The impact of an asteroid would have created a huge crater.

places around the globe, Alvarez and his team discovered that the same high level of iridium is found all over the world. Perhaps something extraterrestrial did cause great changes on earth sixty-five million years ago!

According to Alvarez, this is what happened. An asteroid six miles (9.6 km) wide crashed into the earth, making a huge crater 320 miles (514.9 km) wide. The shock of the impact caused earthquakes and tidal waves. Dust from the pulverized earth was thrown up into the air and formed a dense cloud. This cloud spread and blocked out the light of the sun. The world was in cold darkness for three to six months.

Plants and plankton that needed the sunlight died. The animals that fed on them died also. Many animals could not survive the dip in temperature.

When the dust settled and the sun shone again, a cloud of water vapor remained in the air. It held in the sun's heat, creating a greenhouse effect and greatly warming the earth's atmosphere. Those that had survived the dark and cold were now in a weakened state and could not survive the unbearable heat.

How did some species survive the asteroid catastrophe? Why did pterosaurs disappear and birds flourish? What made some marine animals die out but did not destroy fish or clams? How did mammals survive?

One answer is that furred and feathered creatures had some protection from cold temperatures and from radiation. As plants became more scarce during the time of darkness, birds were able to fly long distances to find new sources of food like scattered seeds and rotting fruit. The fur-protected nocturnal mammals were used to hunting insects in the dark. Small scavengers also had the edge. As The Great Dying continued, their food supply increased.

When the darkness was followed by a heating up of the planet, animals that could hibernate or burrow into the ground to keep cool had the survival advantage. Certainly huge dinosaurs were at a disadvantage. Fish, clams and other creatures that lived in the deep ocean were less exposed to temperature changes and radiation than were those who dwelled near the sur-

◁ **Did an asteroid strike the earth sixty-five million years ago?**

face. Perhaps that is how they survived the catastrophe.

Dying by degrees

Some scientists say that if an asteroid hit the earth, dinosaurs didn't know about it. That is because they were already extinct, as were many other plants and animals. These scientists believe that The Great Dying was not sudden, but gradual. It was caused by a combination of events, none of them coming from outer space.

During the last million years of the Cretaceous Period, the movement of the great land masses caused the levels of oceans to drop. Land that had been under water became dry land. Marine creatures that had lived in shallow water had far fewer habitats.

As the land shifted, it caused changes in the weather. Ocean and air currents changed. Mountains were pushed up, blocking sea breezes from reaching the interior of continents. Inland seas that had kept temperatures in the interior fairly constant drained into the oceans. Volcanoes erupted, filling the air with ash and gases. This led to an air pollution problem that may have led to a greenhouse effect or a damaged ozone layer and climate change.

Later, there was a worldwide cooling trend. Instead of unvarying subtropical weather, the earth experienced more seasonal temperatures. Dino-

▽ The last dinosaurs,
Tyrannosaurus and
Triceratops.

saurs, who had successfully adapted to climate changes for millions of years, could not meet the challenge this time. As one dinosaur hunter said, "Perhaps everything went wrong at the same time."

Paleontologist Robert Bakker believes that when the sea level dropped, it actually opened up migration pathways for dinosaurs and other large animals. Land bridges that had been submerged were now passable. As food sources dried up in one area, dinosaurs and other animals that had evolved in one ecosystem were pressured to move into other ecosystems. By competing with the native species, they upset the balance of the ecosystem.

Perhaps newly arrived plant-eaters stripped the plants that a native species depended upon. Foreign predators may have killed off populations of native plant-eaters. Meanwhile, the exchange of parasites and germs could have wiped out creatures who had built up no immunity to foreign diseases. Contact with a herd of strange dinosaurs may have spelled death for many.

The gradual disappearance of the dinosaur from the fossil record starts in Africa, followed by South America. Sometime after, dinosaurs disappeared from Europe. Only in North America and Mongolia did large numbers of dinosaurs persist for any length of time. The last dinosaurs to disappear were Triceratops and Tyrannosaurus.

As dinosaurs decreased, the number and species of furry mammals increased. The next 200 million years saw the mammals grow larger and begin hunting in the daytime. Herds of plant-eating, hoofed mammals took over the plains. Mammalian predators stalked them. Bats, the flying mammals, took to the air. Some mammals, such as whales and porpoises, returned to the sea. The extinction of the dinosaurs opened doors of opportunity for mammals. Without dinosaur competition, they were finally able to get a foothold in the world. Eventually, one mammal species would dominate the earth and hold the key to the planet's future.

Picture today's dinosaur

What would have happened if dinosaurs had not died out? Humans, of course, would never have had the chance to evolve. But what would the dinosaurs of sixty-five million years ago look like now?

Paleontologist Dale Russell, curious about this very question, studied the remains of the little dinosaur Troödon, a large-brained hunter with keen eyesight. By extending the evolutionary trends that Troödon exhibited in its last few million years, Russell was able to make a model of what the creature would look like now. He calls it the dinosauroid.

The dinosauroid has a large skull to house its large brain. Its neck is short and strong to carry the large head. Like most dinosaurs, it has oval eyes. Without a long neck to balance, the long tail is unnecessary and has disappeared. Its skin is scaly and it has three fingers on each hand.

Mother dinosauroids do not lay eggs but bear live young, so dinosauroids have navels! But because they do not nurse their young as mammals do, dinosauroids have no nipples. They are warm-blooded and probably live in hunting groups. Trends in brain development of Troödon show that dinosauroids may have a language. Perhaps they speak in birdlike calls!

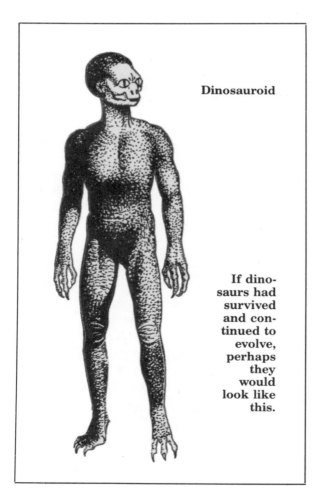

Dinosauroid

If dinosaurs had survived and continued to evolve, perhaps they would look like this.

10

MODERN-DAY DINOSAURS

Are dinosaurs really extinct? For many years scientists believed that sixty-five million years ago the last dinosaur lay down and died. No more baby dinosaurs were born. The giant reptiles that once ruled the earth vanished, leaving only fossils as a testament to their existence.

Now many dinosaur detectives insist that the dinosaurs never really died out. In fact, they believe that dinosaur descendants are living all around us now. We see them and hear them everyday. They are birds!

The evidence

For some time scientists have noticed that a group of theropod dinosaurs, called coelurosaurs [SEE-ler-o-sawrs], were amazingly birdlike. If you compare the hind feet and scaly legs of some of these dinosaurs, like Ornitholestes, Deinonychus and Compsagnathus, with modern-day birds, the similarities are striking. But the resemblance between dinosaur and bird is more than skin deep.

When paleontologist John Ostrom studied Deinonychus, he found that the bones of the ankle, hip, toes, feet, thighs and hand reminded him of another Mesozoic creature he had just finished studying—Archaeopteryx, the first bird. The truth is that if fossils of

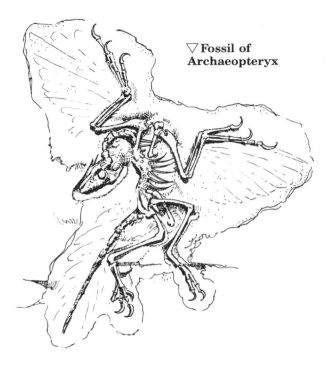

▽ **Fossil of Archaeopteryx**

Archeopteryx had not clearly shown the impression of feathers, the primitive bird would have been classified as a dinosaur. Could it be that Archeopteryx is what scientists call the "missing link" in the evolution of dinosaur into bird?

Ancient wing

Archaeopteryx [ar-kee-OP-ter-ix], or "ancient wing," lived during the Jurassic Period, 140 million years ago. The few fossils that have been discovered are in lithographic limestone from West Germany. This limestone produces fossils with such fine detail that it is possible to examine minute features of a single feather from this remarkable winged creature.

But the wonderful wings did not enable Archaeopteryx to fly. It lacked a bird's broad, flat breast bone where flight muscles are attached. Flapping like a chicken, it could run speedily along the ground, snapping at flying insects, trying to trap them between its wings. If Archaeopteryx trapped its prey, it could grab the insect with its three-clawed hands and pop the morsel into its tooth-lined beak. Perhaps as this first bird ran and leaped after dragonflies and cicadas, the feathered wings held it aloft for a second or two.

Another theory has Archeaopteryx as a tree dweller, climbing up with its clawed hands and feet to a height safe from ground-dwelling predators, and then using its wings to glide from tree to tree or to the ground to feed. Scientists who study the origin of flight debate Archaeopteryx lifestyle, but they do agree that there was much about the first bird that was very unbirdlike and very like the two-legged theropods.

For instance, Archaeopteryx, like a coelurosaur, had a long, bony tail and tiny teeth in its long snout. Its pelvis, shoulder and forearm are more like those of a reptile than a bird. Like a coelurosaur, it had a long, flexible neck, large eyes and a large brain.

So was Archaeopteryx a dinosaur with feathers or a very dinosaurlike bird? Many experts believe that Archeaopteryx is a bit of both, the link between dinosaur and bird. It is possible that the more than 8,000 species of birds on the earth today descended from small, big-brained coelurosaurs.

▷**Archaeopteryx**

Feathers and warm-bloodedness

Why did dinosaur reptile scales gradually evolve into feathers on Archaeopteryx? Was it because feathers kept the dinosaur warm? A small, active theropod could use a layer of feath-

74

ers if it was warm-blooded. But feathers would be a handicap to an ectothermic reptile who needed to absorb the heat of the sun by basking. The fossil feathers are the clue. The answer—Archeaopteryx was probably warm-blooded, an endotherm.

Dinosaur detectives like John Ostrom, who believes that dinosaurs and birds belong on the same branch of the

▽ **Hesperornis**

family tree, have suggested that Archaeopteryx inherited warm-bloodedness from the coelurosaurs. Perhaps little Compsognathus was warm-blooded and had feathers, too!

Birds with teeth

During the Early Cretaceous Period, birds appeared that were close to modern birds in structure except that, like coelurosaurs, their long jaws were lined with sharp teeth.

Ichthyornis [ik-thee-ORN-is], or "fish bird," probably looked like a small seagull. Its broad breast bone and shoulder bone indicate that it was a strong flyer. It was a fishing bird and lived on the shores of the inland sea in what is now Kansas.

Hesperornis [hes-per-ORN-is], or "western bird," on the other hand, could not fly at all. Its wings were too tiny and weak for flight. It had powerful swimming legs, however. Perhaps this four-foot-high (1.2 m) swimming and diving bird used its wings for steering, just like a penguin does, when it dove beneath the water to grab fish with its toothy beak.

▷ **Ichthyornis**

Class Aves

As more evidence is found to support the dinosaur/bird connection, some scientists have suggested that the classification of dinosaurs and birds be changed. Paleontologists Robert Bakker has proposed that a new class called the Dinosauria be created consisting of three orders: Saurischia, Ornithischia and Aves (birds).

Of course, there are some bird studiers who would not like to see the Class Aves fall beneath the Dinosauria. Those who feel strongly about the relationship between birds and dinosaurs have made a counter proposal. They suggest that the carnivorous dinosaurs be placed in the Class Aves. In other words, Allosaurus, Tyrannosaurus, Deinonychus, Compsognathus and Ornitholestes would all be classified as birds!

Whether these classification changes are ever made, scientists are convinced that some dinosaurs are close relatives of birds, if not their direct ancestors. The dinosaurs who suc-cessfully dominated the earth for 140 million years were not wiped out, but left a line that has continued to this day.

In a way, it is comforting to know that those mighty giants of the Mesozoic Era who thundered, galloped, plodded, shuffled and scuttled across the land have not disappeared. If we look up, we can see them soaring through the sky!

GLOSSARY

aestivate–sleep during dry seasons

ammonites–extinct sea mollusks in the same family as squid

angiosperm–flowering plant

ankylosaurs–family of dinosaurs with bony armor

archosaurs–group of animals that includes crocodiles, pterosaurs and dinosaurs

asteroid–one of thousands of tiny planets that revolve around the sun between the orbits of Mars and Jupiter

Aves–birds

bipedal–walks on two feet

carnosaur–a large theropod

ceratopsians–family of plant-eating, four-legged, horned dinosaurs

coelurosaur–a small theropod

coprolites–fossilized animal droppings

Cretaceous Period–third period in the Mesozoic Era, 135 to sixty-five million years ago

cycad–a Mesozoic plant that resembled a palm tree with a thick trunk and tough leaves

dinosaurs–a group of land reptiles that appeared about 215 million years ago and became extinct about sixty-five million years ago. Unlike other reptiles, they walked with their legs under their bodies.

dinosauroid–an imaginary picture of what the dinosaur Troödon would look like today if it had continued to evolve

ectotherm–an animal that depends on an outside source of heat to maintain its body temperature; a cold-blooded animal

endocranial cast–a mold of the inside of the brain case

endotherm–an animal that can make heat inside its body; a warm-blooded animal

fossils–remains of prehistoric plants and animals that have turned to stone

gastroliths–belly stones swallowed by an animal in order to grind up plant matter in the stomach

geology–the study of rocks

ginkgo–a nonflowering plant that was common during the Mesozoic Era and was a source of food for many plant-eating dinosaurs. All but one species of ginkgo are extinct today

Gondwanaland–great southern continent of the Jurassic Period made up of Africa, India, South America, Antarctica and Australia

greenhouse effect–a heating up that occurs when the sun's rays hit the Earth but the heat is not allowed to radiate and escape the Earth's atmosphere

gymnosperm–nonflowering plants like the sequoia or pine

hadrosaurs–large plant-eating dinosaurs that are called "duckbills" because of the shape of their snouts

ichnology–the study of footprints

ichthyosaurs–large fish-shaped reptiles that swam in the sea during the Mesozoic Era

iridium–an element found in meteorites and in the Earth's core

Jurassic Period–second period in the Mesozoic Era from 200 million years ago to 135 million years ago

Laurasia–great northern continent of the Jurassic Period made up of North America, Europe and Asia

mosasaur–sharp-toothed, sea-going reptile of the Mesozoic Era

Mesozoic Era–period of time from 225 to sixty-five million years ago